Glory Lightl

A TRIBUTE TO BRIAN STATHAM

Compiled and Edited by
Rev. Malcolm G. Lorimer

The Parrs Wood Press
MANCHESTER

First Published 2001

THE PARRS WOOD PRESS
St Wilfrid's Enterprise Centre
Royce Road, Manchester, M15 5BJ
www.parrswoodpress.com

08600340

© Rev. Malcolm G. Lorimer 2001

ISBN: 1 903158 22 2

This book was produced by Andrew Searle, Helen Faulkner and Russell Hayes of The Parrs Wood Press and Printed in Great Britain by:

MFP Design and Print
Longford Trading Estate
Thomas Street
Stretford
Manchester M32 0JT

For Audrey and Brian's family

ABOUT THE AUTHOR

Rev. Malcolm G. Lorimer is a Methodist Minister who is Superintendent of the Sale Circuit with pastoral responsibility for The Avenue Methodist Church. He was minister for 12 years in Moss Side, Manchester. He is chaplain to Lancashire County Cricket Club and has edited the Lancashire Year Book since 1987 as well as editing the Benefit Brochures for John Abrahams, Mike Watkinson and Graham Lloyd. He was born in Haworth, Yorkshire, but says of his love of Lancashire: "I believe in the power of conversion"! For a number of years he was also Hon. Librarian at the club. He has written books on Lancashire Cricketers, Lancashire Cricket Grounds and Cyril Washbrook. He is interested in the links between Cricket and Christianity and is currently Chairman of The Association of Cricket Statisticians and Historians. His interests include collecting cricket memorabilia, theatre and crime novels. Despite an early altercation with a cricket roller at the age of seven (which deprived him of his front two teeth), he has loved the game of cricket and one of his treasured moments was taking the wickets of four clergymen with four successive balls!

ACKNOWLEDGEMENTS

My thanks to all the players and collegues of Brian who have so readily contributed articles to this book. To the Lancashire Former Players Association and Lancashire CCC for all their help. I would like to thank Keith Hayhurst, Don Ambrose, Tony Sheldon, Geoff Wilde, Mick Pope, Les Hatton, William Powell for help with photos and profiles. For Lancashire CCC, David Dawson and Notts CCC Library for photographs and drawings by Arthur Dooley and Roy Ullyett. To Sally Bates for typesetting the manuscript, Charles Oliver, David Baggett, Ken Thomas who helped with proofreading. Andy Searle at The Parrs Wood Press for making this book possible and his encouragement. For The Independent, Sunday Times, Manchester Evening News, The Guardian, Wisden Cricket Monthly, Playfair Cricket Monthly and The Cricketer for permission to reprint articles. Cricinfo for allowing me to reproduce items from the Internet. Lastly, but my no means the least, my thanks to Audrey Statham for allowing me to use photographs of Brian and encouragement with the book.

CONTENTS

FOREWORD

We all need heroes: men and women we can look up to, those who do great deeds that the rest of us only dream about. They are larger than life and illuminate our lives, whether it be on the battlefield, the unclimbed mountain or the sports-field heroes are found and acclaimed. They don't set out to be heroic but find it thrust upon them through their great achievements. By any standard or measure, Brian Statham was a hero to people in Lancashire and England. They followed his career and could only stand back in awe and amazement. But the reason for this book is much more than the celebration of a hero.

There are some heroes who will tell you of their greatness; they write books and go on chat shows extolling their own virtues. Others will push themselves to the front and trample over their fellows. Some will expect privileges and not want to mix with ordinary people. Brian Statham was never part of all that, his quiet temperament and affable nature was an example to young players. Brian's modesty was part of his greatness. He came from a humble background and the show of public affection and acclaim he took in his stride. He conquered the world of cricket but fame never separated Brian from his fellows, from the ordinary man in the street. This perhaps is a better understanding of greatness. Many heroes have feet of clay and disappoint away from the sports field or in their private lives. Brian did not disappoint.

The title of this book was inspired by Michael Henderson, Cricket Correspondent of the Daily Telegraph. In his obituary of Brian he said, "Statham brought to the game that most precious of human qualities: glory, lightly worn. He added a verse to the eternal chorus, and must be remembered."

"Glory, Lightly Worn" for me epitomises Brian.

When I conducted the funeral for Brian Statham in June 2000 I was particularly moved by what was said about him by his cricketing colleagues. Afterwards I decided to produce this book as a tribute to him and contact his former colleagues for their appreciations, anecdotes and stories.

I was amazed at the number of people who replied and how willing they were to contribute. This says much about the way Brian was regarded by his fellow players. I would like to thank all those who so readily replied to my request.

There is more to say of Brian's greatness. There was something else more important to him than cricket: his family. They were so precious to him and so supportive of his career. I am pleased that Audrey has read the text and provided many of the photos. At the service last June I asked Brian's children to write something about their father. I wasn't prepared for what they wrote.

Often the children of the famous have difficulty relating to them but they paid the greatest tribute that could be paid and certainly the greatest in this book. They said: "He was a great cricketer but a greater father." This was a wonderful tribute and one I am sure Brian would have treasured that above the greatest sporting accolade.

I hope this book does justice to someone who was not just a great cricketer, a hero and sporting legend, but a great man.

Rev. Malcolm G. Lorimer August 2001.

PART ONE

Statham the Man

BRIAN STATHAM

· BORN GORTON, MANCHESTER, 17TH JUNE 1930

* MADE DEBUT FOR LANCASHIRE ON HIS 20TH BIRTHDAY
v KENT AT OLD TRAFFORD IN 1950.

* AWARDED COUNTY CAP IN HIS FIRST SEASON 1950.

* FLOWN OUT TO AUSTRALIA TO JOIN THE M.C.C. TEAM AT THE
END OF HIS FIRST SEASON IN COUNTY CRICKET.

* MADE DEBUT FOR ENGLAND v NEW ZEALAND AT
CHRISTCHURCH IN 1951.

* PLAYED FOR LANCASHIRE FROM 1950 TO 1968.

A TRIBUTE TO BRIAN STATHAM

* CAPTAINED LANCASHIRE FROM 1965 TO 1967.

* TOOK MORE WICKETS FOR LANCASHIRE (1,816)
THAN ANY OTHER BOWLER
AND ALSO THE MOST IN FIRST-CLASS CRICKET (2,260).

* TOOK 100 WICKETS IN A SEASON 13 TIMES
- THE MOST FOR A LANCASHIRE BOWLER.

* HEADED THE LANCASHIRE BOWLING AVERAGES FOR
16 SUCCESSIVE SEASONS (A UNIQUE RECORD).

* TOOK 252 WICKETS IN TEST CRICKET AND BECAME THE SEC-
OND ENGLAND BOWLER TO TAKE 250 WICKETS IN TESTS.

* TOOK 15 FOR 89 IN A MATCH V WARWICKSHIRE AT COVENTRY
IN 1957 INCLUDING A CAREER BEST 8 FOR 34.

* TOOK 3 HAT TRICKS IN FIRST -CLASS CRICKET.

* PLAYED IN 70 TEST MATCHES FOR ENGLAND
- MORE THAN ANY OTHER LANCASHIRE PLAYER AT THE TIME.

* WISDEN CRICKETER OF THE YEAR IN 1955.

* SERVED ON THE LANCASHIRE COMMITTEE 1969 TO 1991.

* AWARDED THE CBE AND HONORARY CRICKET MEMBERSHIP
OF THE MCC FOR HIS SERVICES TO CRICKET.

* AWARDED HONORARY DOCTORATE
BY LANCASTER UNIVERSITY IN 1991.

* DIED ON 10TH JUNE 2000 AGED 69.

"George"

by John Arlott

Brian Statham, like his right-arm fast bowling, was straight and honest. No professional cricketer has been more universally respected and his nickname "George", was a fitting tribute to his gentlemanly and scrupulously fair nature. His popularity in no way decreased his effectiveness as an extremely accurate and skilful pace bowler. Tall (6ft) and exceptionally lithe and supple (he was also called "The Whippet"), he had a beautifully rhythmic and smoothly accelerated run-up, culminating in a high flowing action and follow through. His lissom movements were accentuated by his being double-jointed; when removing his sweater he would reach the back ribbing by coiling his right arm over his right shoulder more than half way down his spine. He was so accurate that on soft turf the marks where he pitched were usually grouped like rifle shots around a bull's-eye. Allied to this phenomena; control was his ability to move the ball either way off the seam. For almost a decade his partnerships with Tyson and Trueman enabled England to recover from the frequent shortfalls produced by erratic batting. His probing accuracy was the ideal foil for his partners' more varied and volatile pace and proved a major factor in their success. He was at his peak in 1954-55 and his speed in that Australian summer was not far short of Tyson's. He was the most undemonstrative of fast bowlers; a studious technician rather than a flamboyant artist. A superb mover in the field with a formidable throw, he seldom had the energy or opportunity to demonstrate his ability as a left-handed batsman. He was a shrewd and popular Lancashire captain for three seasons (1965-67).

"If my son became a professional cricketer, I hope he would be like Brian Statham". The words are Colin Cowdrey's: but the sentiment is shared by every man who ever played a game of cricket with that pleasant, sound cricketer, John Brian Statham.

Probably the most suitable appointment for this wise, willing and considerate man would be that of perpetual captain of the Players against the Gentlemen. For if, as a wit once suggested, not all the Gentlemen are players. "George", beyond all doubt, was a great player and one of nature's gentlemen.

From *Playfair Cricket Monthly*, April 1962

My Most Memorable Match

I bowled throughout South Africa's second innings without a break in the Lord's Test of 1955 and my figures at the end were: 29 overs, 12 maidens, 7 wickets, 39 runs. The analysis would have been even better but for a couple of blatant catches being given not out by the umpire! The ball moved about a lot off the seam and we rushed South Africa out for 111 to win the match by 71 runs.

My Childhood Bowling Hero

"Ted" McDonald, the Australian who played for Nelson in the Lancashire League and then qualified to represent Lancashire. He had one of the most graceful run-ups of any fast bowler and was so light and elegant on his way in to deliver the ball that he rarely left any foot marks even on the softest ground. I grew up surrounded by people talking about his achievements and in particular how his pace bowling had helped Lancashire win three County championships. When confronted by a class batsman - a Hobbs or a Bradman - they say he used to increase his speed to a lightning-fast pace yet losing nothing in his elegance. I would have loved to have watched him at his peak.

My Childhood Batting Hero

Sir Donald Bradman, fleet of foot and possessing an uncanny knack of finding gaps in the tightest field with a full range of shots. His career average of 95.14 and his Test average of 99.94 says it all. He was the greatest run-maker the game has ever known and he could score big totals on any wicket and against the finest bowlers in the world of all speeds and varieties. He could drive, cut, hook, sweep - you name it and the shot was in his repertoire.

My idea of the Perfect Bowler

It has surely got to be Sydney Barnes, who was a perfectionist capable of taking advantage of any ground conditions. There was no such thing as a "good batting wicket" when he was operating with the ball. He had immaculate control of length, direction and swing, constantly making the batsmen play and demanding the best from his fielders. His 189 wickets in 27 Tests at an average of 16.43 are figures that reveal just how deadly accurate he was against the top batsmen.

My idea of the Perfect Batsman

Bradman, of course, and Sir Frank Worrell. Frank was graceful, had good defensive technique, was a beautiful timer of the ball, possessed patience and was prepared to work hard. When necessary he had the shots to take any attack apart.

Both he and "The Don" had the exceptional power of concentration that sets the great batsmen apart.

Brian Statham's Ten Greatest New Ball Partners

1 Harold Larwood and Bill Voce (England
2 Ray Lindwall and Keith Miller (Australia)
3 Dennis Lillee and Jeff Thomson (Australia)
4 Wes Hall and Charlie Griffith (West Indies)
5 Michael Holding and Andy Roberts (West Indies)
6 Alec Bedser and Peter Loader (England)
7 Peter Heine and Neil Adcock (South Africa)
8 Alan Davidson and Graham McKenzie (Australia)
9 Peter Pollock and Mike Procter (South Africa)
10 Les Jackson and Cliff Gladwin (England)

"I did not have the good fortune to see Larwood and Voce in action but from the stories I have been told by their contemporaries they must have been sheer dynamite together. I have selected two great County combinations - Bedser and Loader, who did so much to make Surrey supreme in the 1950s, and Jackson and Gladwin, who wrecked the best batting sides when they got them on those green wickets of Derbyshire. A pair I would loved to have seen in harness at their peak are my old partners Fred Trueman and Frank Tyson. That would have been quite a spectacle, except for the batsmen on the receiving end!"

From *The Book of Cricket Lists*, Edited by Norman Giller

The Truth about Trueman by Brian Statham

Half the people of the North seem to be convinced that Freddie Trueman and I are rivals. I suppose that logically that's a fair enough assumption - we are both fast bowlers, we come from those cat-and-dog counties Yorkshire and Lancashire.

Yet, in fact, nothing is further from the truth. We are the best of pals, and I don't give tuppence how many wickets he takes. Admittedly, if he's knocking them over at one end, I might go a little bit harder myself to see if I can chip in with a couple. But that's just a normal reaction. I would do that whoever was bowling with me.

But the popular picture of two surly fast bowlers, envying each other's success and not speaking to each other, is a million miles off beam. I don't care if Fred picks up all ten when we are playing for England, as long as I am satisfied in myself that I have bowled as well as I can.

As for not speaking .. we jabber away like a couple of old women over a pot of tea. And, in all the time we have been playing and touring together, we have never had a cross word.

I should think Fred feels the same way about bowling with me. We are both much more interested in the result of the match than in our own achievements. I have seen him with a 'ton' (a hundred runs) against his name overnight, and the only effect it has had is for him to come out and do his darnedest to improve matters next morning.

Fred, with his hands-on-hips postures and his glares, has a reputation for being a temperamental character. And rightly so.

Compared with his earlier days, he is a well-mannered angel. But he still has flashes of temper and occasional outbursts of language that would burn the hair off a coconut. I don't take any notice. They don't mean anything - at least, not anything lasting.

He's a likeable chap with a heart as big as a soup-plate. If he likes you he would do anything for you - except one thing. He won't lend anybody money. That's his principle and he stands firmly by it. He wouldn't even lend money to me, and I suppose we are closer than any other two players in the England dressing-room.

I have always enjoyed bowling with Fred, and I reckon myself lucky to have been in harness with him for such a long time (we first came together in the West Indies on the tour of 1953-4). It's a help when you know the bowler at the other end is trying as hard as you are.

Yet, terrific fighter that he is, his bowling still depends to a certain extent on that fiery temperament of his. He can be a thoroughly nasty proposition sometimes in even the easiest of conditions. It depends on his mood.

And the batsmen themselves have a certain amount of control over how he bowls to them. If they play him well and firmly, then Fred looks upon it as an honourable duel, even going so far as to give grudging credit.

But if they play at him and miss a lot, then woe betide them! Batsmen not batting well, Fred expects to see go. And if the luck runs with them and they stay, then Fred becomes thoroughly angry and gets stuck into them. That is his attitude to the game.

You never get to know anybody properly in this game of cricket until you have lived with them for a while. Fred and I found we hit it off so well together - we shared rooms on the last trip to the West Indies - because we are similar in some ways, unlikely as that may seem to spectators watching from a distance.

He is a restless sort of person, not fond of going to bed early. I am like that, too. When we had to bed down early during the Tests we would read to all hours of the night.

Yes, we share much common ground, and we like bowling together, but we have got our differences too. For instance, we quire often differ on how we think we can get a batsman out. Fred might go for a leg-stick attack while I fancy the off-side. It doesn't mean that either of us is wrong, merely that we approach our problem differently. After all, I have yet to meet the batsman who is infallible on any stump.

Again, it will surprise those who still class Fred as something of a wild bowler (so wrongly!) that he is a deep thinker about the game. He has a prodigious memory for batsmen's weaknesses, details of matches and even scores.

And on Yorkshire's cricket history he is a regular one-man brains trust. He can tell you details of their championship-winning sides from the year dot, when players retired, their runs, wickets and anything you like to ask.

Fred Trueman now is a complete fast bowler. His erratic days are behind him and his control now is better than most. He does most of his work through the air, swinging the ball considerably. He cuts one back off the seam occasionally, but he is essentially an out-swing bowler.

He describes himself as a middle-and-leg bowler, which I presume means that he starts his swing on the middle- and leg- stumps. His bowling, in fact, is a complete contrast to my own, for my target is invariably the off-stump, with the ball doing little or nothing through the air but moving either way off the seam. In addition, Freddie is inclined to pitch a shorter length than I do.

But he has more or less perfected a good flat Yorker, which is good theory - get them on the back foot and then throw in the Yorker.

Yet to talk of Fred in terms of theory is not right. He is essentially a human, full-blooded cricketer, full of moods, whims and brilliance.

Typical of him was the incident at Johannesburg in 1960, when we were playing together in a private tour that was full of good fun and good cricket. The number-one requirement of that trip was to provide entertainment. And, as you might guess, Fred did his bit to the full.

When this gag was dreamed up, he was batting with Tom Graveney. During the tea-break, Tom came up to Fred and told him that Jackie McGlew, who usually bowled leg-breaks, was coming on to bowl after tea. As McGlew had received as many bouncers from Fred as any man, it was reckoned it would be a good gag if he bowled one at Fred.

Said Tom, "Jackie says it will be second ball after tea, so watch our for it. It will go down the leg-side and you are to swish your bat after it has gone by - as if it is too fast for you."

"O.K." said Fred. "Anything for a laugh."

Sure enough, second ball after tea, McGlew, who had been bowling slow off a six-yard run, suddenly turned and marched miles back in this giant Wanderers ground. The crowd hummed, and then this tiny figure turned and hurtled back towards the stumps to let go a bumper, the genuine article.

The only thing wrong with the plan was that the ball, instead of whistling harmlessly down the leg-side, was pitched on the middle stump and came close to nailing our Fred, as he nearly ducked into the line of it.

I have never seen such indignation in one man in all my life. His hands were jabbed on his hips, and he bristled up the wicket at McGlew. The crowd loved it.

Fred was outraged when he got back to the pavilion. He was absolutely certain McGlew had laid a trap for him. I talked a long, long time to him, pointing out that it was an accident and that a chap like McGlew wouldn't be able to control the direction of a bouncer.

Even in the end I don't think Fred was completely convinced.

You will hear a lot of nonsense talked about Fred Trueman. He has been found guilty of far more things than he ever did. He has taken the blame and never squealed back.

Unlike most of the critics, I know him. And I could not wish for a better friend.

From *Flying Bails*, by Brian Statham, Stanley Paul 1961

Neither of us were worried who got the wickets as long as we were in our favourite position - our feet up watching England bat.
Brian Statham, recalling his fast-bowling partnership with Fred Trueman

---

A TRIBUTE TO BRIAN STATHAM

Brian Statham being honoured by Lancaster University

Your Royal Highness and Chancellor:

Those present today who love cricket and cherish its great heroes will understand the more than sense of awe that I feel in presenting to you, on behalf of the Senate, Brian Statham, for the award of the degree of Doctor of Law, Honoris Causa. With this award the University of the red rose county fittingly honours a great Lancastrian.

Brian Statham was born in 1930 the son of a dentist, from whom, one supposes he may have inherited some of his later facility in rooting our recalcitrant stumps. Oddly, in view of his later distinction, he showed little early enthusiasm for cricket. At school it was a convenient way of escaping from the classroom and later, in the RAF, it became an equally efficacious way of avoiding office fatigues. Indeed, he had only seen one day of county cricket when he joined Lancashire in 1950. This led to interesting misunderstandings. His debut was against Kent, whose team included the great batsman, Arthur Fagg. As they went onto the field the legendary Cyril Washbrook said to him, "Don't bowl short to Fagg." The problem was that Mr Statham did not know which of the two batsmen was Arthur Fagg and didn't like to ask. Of course he promptly bowled a short ball to Fagg who, to complete the saga, equally promptly mishit it and skied a catch. Washbrook, he records, gave him a funny old look.

Mr Statham, of course went on to become one of the greatest of cricketers. He played over 500 matches and took well over 2000 wickets. He played in 70 Tests and took 252 wickets, a total which, with luck might be reached collectively by the current England attack by the end of the millennium. In 1963 he became the holder of the world record for wickets taken in Test matches, a record later taken from him by his great colleague, Fred Trueman.

Although no mean batsman he never scored a century, an event dreamt of by tail-end bowlers with the fervour with which ham comedians dream of playing Hamlet. He nearly made it in 1955 against Leicestershire. On that day he was told to go in and throw the bat - an expression which had a slightly different meaning in those less temperamental times. He had scored 62 runs in 30 minutes when a message was sent in by his captain, Cyril Washbrook. It read, to quote a carefully expurgated version, "What are you doing, you fool. I want you fresh for the last half hour. Get out." And, not being Geoffrey Boycott, Statham promptly demolished his own stumps. But one institution did pay proper tribute to his batting prowess and that was the University of Lancaster, who wished to test empirically the hypothesis that a ball could be hit onto the A6 from the road-side pitch. Statham demonstrated the truth of this hypothesis with one mighty blow - hence the nets in front of the university - wrongly believed by many who pass by to be a means of preventing disaffected students from eloping.

Statistics do not capture the reasons why Mr Statham is revered by all true lovers of sport. He belongs to and exemplifies an attitude to the playing of games that is, alas, increasingly rare. That attitude combines modesty with a commitment to fair play and honesty of effort. Mr Statham believes that batsmen should unhesitatingly walk when they know that they are out, and that bowlers should attack the stumps rather than the batsman. He is unfailingly generous in his admiration for the achievements of others, most notably for the achievements of his wife Audrey who kept a family together during his long absences on tour and who gave his domestic life such stability.

Your Royal Highness and Chancellor:

Today, then, we pay tribute to a legendary figure in Lancashire and a legendary figure in the history of a beautiful and historic game. For millions of people his name conjures golden memories of a time when, with Statham at one end and Trueman at the other, every game offered hope. More than that, he is a reminder to an age that needs such reminders, that extra-ordinary talent can be combined with a fundamental modesty and decency. For that he has won the unreserved admiration of countless cricket watchers, to whom his skills and achievements gave so much pleasure. It is therefore my great honour on behalf of the Senate, to present to you John Brian Statham CBE, as eminently worthy of the award of the degree of Doctor of Laws, Honoris Causa.

First Impressions

By Brian Statham

You may be surprised to learn that my first impressions of cricket were that I preferred tennis! Until the summer of 1949 I had never thought of playing county cricket; yet within five years I was to play against the chosen best of all the cricketing counties.

I always played sport for sheer enjoyment. This was particularly true during the two seasons I was playing with Denton West. I enjoyed bowling more than anything else, and match after match I was allowed to carry on in my own way. I never bothered about "style", but rhythm and co-ordination I did bother about.

Of course, I have always been thrilled by good bowling figures. Success does, indeed, breed success. In a league match against Barton Hall I took 9-17 and in another match 8-15. The main thing successes did for me was to increase continually my enthusiasm for the game as a whole.

There have been times when I bowled better without taking wickets than when I returned good figures. Unless taken over a long period, or in relation to all circumstances of weather, wicket and opposition in a particular match, bowling figures mean little.

I seldom study bowling figures. This, I suggest, is good practice at all times. Too much attention to figures and averages can make you feel too self-satisfied at times and give you stomach ulcers on the other and more frequent occasions.

The first money I ever received for playing cricket was during the match when I took 8-15. Collections were taken if a bowler obtained seven wickets or a hat-trick. For my wickets I had a collection of five shillings and fourpence. The collection worked out at eightpence a wicket! For once I was interested in averages!

The collection was fourpence more than my prize for winning the league averages with 96 wickets at a cost of six runs each!

Written by Brian Statham for a Foreword
for the 'Cricket Record Book of Lancashire' by Malcolm Lorimer

TRIBUTES

Brian Statham - a cricketing legend in his own lifetime.
Sir Fred Pontin

His own quality was his ability to move the ball off the seam giving him great accuracy hence we had the finest combination of our time!
Godfrey Evans

Brian was the most loyal colleague and the fairest opponent.
Colin Cowdrey

Trueman and Statham - what a double act! Fred was the comic, and Brian the straight man - and nobody bowled straighter. A formidable team.
Leslie Crowther

To me as a schoolboy, Brian Statham was the ultimate thoroughbred fast bowler - a magnificent run up, fast and threatening and he never bowled a wasted ball.
Henry Kelly

No-one could wish to travel with a better tourist and companion. Add to this he never gave up trying, who could ask for more.
Alec Bedser

No captain could wish for a better man in his team.
Sir Leonard Hutton

No Test bowler tried harder, complained less or kept his temper better than "George" Statham. What a great example he sets us all.
Ted Dexter

Brian epitomised to me all we hope for in our sports heroes - ability, loyalty and good sportsmanship, all of the highest.
Reg Hayter

A TRIBUTE TO BRIAN STATHAM

To watch Brian running up to the wicket was like watching a gazelle taking off. A picture of purposeful elegance.
Bill Pertwee

As a youngster the names Statham and Trueman went together for me like the lion and the unicorn; synonymous with British pride - and Brian's name was the watchword for relentless accuracy.
Peter Baxter

"George" - Great bowler, Big heart and the longest suffering feet in the game!
Richie Benaud

A marvellously accurate bowler - captaincy was easy with him on your side.
Peter May

He always got me out. The nicest bloke in the game. One of the finest of all quick bowlers.
Tom Graveney

They simply do not come any better than Brian, both on the field and off. He was the ideal tourist.
Trevor Bailey

Fred and Ginger, Fred and Brian; they're inseparable. I'm delighted to pay tribute to the other half of one of the all-time great partnerships.
Rory Bremner

Brian Statham was a master of his craft; a true professional and a cricketer admired the world over.
John Bromley

By George, England could use his like today!
Sir Tim Rice

My salutations to a great cricketer and a great bloke.
Peter West

He was straight both as a man and a bowler. The perfect professional.
Brian Johnston

No professional cricketer has been more universally respected and his nickname "George" was a fitting tribute to his gentlemanly and scrupulously fair nature.
Bill Frindall

Every schoolboy has to have their sporting heroes but two playing for England must be truly memorable. They were Brian Statham and Fred Trueman.
Lord Lichfield

...and to see him and Fred Trueman in full flight was a sight for sore eyes.
Don Wilson

There is only one "George" - a friend both on and off the field.
Raman Subba Row

Great cricketers have always had courage, determination and skill, that is why Brian Statham is one of the very great players of his time.
Denis Thatcher

The most accurate quick bowler I ever had the misfortune to face.
Peter Parfitt

It is impossible for me to be there in anything but spirit, since Australia is a long way away. I shall always treasure, however, the joy of bowling at the opposite end to Brian for England in the 1950s.
Frank Tyson

I am sorry not to be with you tonight, Brian, but I have a concert at Wembley. I do, however, wish you every success. Watching you bowl always gave me the greatest pleasure.
From Sir Elton John at Brian Statham's Tribute Dinner

"Which living person do you most admire?"
"Brian Statham, for his dignity in both success and adversity."
Howard Davies, Director-General of the CBI

Sir Matt Busby

One of the most distinguished and successful football managers ever. He was born in Bellshill, Lanarkshire. After a comparatively undistinguished playing career with Manchester City and Liverpool, he became manager of Manchester United in 1945. Almost immediately the club won the FA Cup in 1948 and the League shortly afterwards, Rebuilding the team, he seemed likely to bring the European Cup to Britain for the first time in 1958 but his young side was largely wiped out in an air crash at Munich airport. He himself was severely injured, but patiently reconstructed the side until European Cup success eventually came in 1968. He died in 1994.

When I first heard the name of Brian Statham mentioned in a sporting context it was as a prospective soccer star. The "scouting" report which reached my office came from Roger Byrne who reached the heights as an England international full-back.

Roger and Brian had been friends for some years. They played in amateur football together and, at that time, we were anxious to build up our junior strength. We were short of wingers and Byrne, who had an uncanny instinct for judging playing ability, asked me if I would be interested in a young player about whom he was very enthusiastic.

The result was that Brian was invited to come along to Old Trafford for a trial. He did not take up the offer because his heart was set on a cricket career. Can you wonder that since then I have watched his rise to the pinnacle of cricketing greatness with particular interest?

Whenever I have seen him racing into action in his whites, I have often wondered whether he would have reached the first-class grade as a winger His graceful running, commendable stamina, fighting spirit and, lastly his sportsmanship, are all assets which coupled with the ability he had as a teenager for the "big ball game", would have qualified him for professional football.

Brian was recognised throughout the world of sport as a truly great cricketer. His accuracy, incredible speed and zest for the sport have won him international acclaim. The record books will always tell the on-field story. But Brian remained a most, unassuming family man,. If one may be permitted to put it in soccer parlance, Brian was a "player's player".

That praise cannot be bettered in professional sport, for to be respected as well as feared is a considerable achievement, especially in team games, Brian we salute you!

Written in 1961 for Brian's Benefit Brochure

PART TWO

Statham of Lancashire

In the nets at Old Trafford, 1951

Graham Atkinson

A Yorkshire born opening batsman with a very sound method, he played for Somerset between 1954-66 and was the youngest player to score 2,000 runs in a season. He scored over 14,000 runs for the county before he left to join Lancashire in 1967 for whom he played in 62 matches and scored 2,468 runs with five centuries. When he retired he played for Crompton before going into Rugby League administration with Salford.

My earliest memory of Brian was not, unusually, related to an exceptional bowling analysis. I had joined Lancashire, from Somerset, in 1967 and early on travelled to Hove where Sussex batted through three sessions. We came off the field and Brian remarked "Ee, that were a bloody hard day" as he slumped in his chair, downed a pint in one and kicked off his boots. Turning to the dressing room attendant, he asked for another pint. "No make that two!" he said. "George" had given his all and was shattered. He was 37 years old at the time.

Bob Barber

Bob Barber was born in Withington, Manchester and made his debut for Lancashire in 1954 when still only 18 and was midway between Ruthin College and Cambridge University. In 1960 he became captain of Lancashire getting off to a flying start with two victories over Yorkshire.

Bob was a superb all-round cricketer. An attacking left-handed batsman, a right arm leg-break bowler and an excellent close to the wicket fielder. He also captained the side in 1961 and then played one more season under Joe Blackledge before leaving to join Warwickshire.

He played in 155 matches in his nine seasons at Old Trafford, scoring 6,760 runs at an average of 28.28 and taking 152 wickets at 31.36 runs each.

At Edgbaston, caution gave way to attack and he became one of the most attractive batsmen in the country. He played 28 times for England with a top score of 185 at Sydney, one of the greatest innings in Ashes history. An adventurous cricketer, highly intelligent and independent, he sacrificed cricket for a business career whilst still in his batting prime. He now lives in Switzerland.

I was a schoolboy when, in 1954, I played my first match for Lancashire; Brian was playing in that team. He was playing for England when I played in my first Test match. He was a member of the Lancashire team over the two years 1960/61 when I captained the side and I think I played with him in his last Test match for England in 1965.

At no time can I ever recall a batsman dominating his bowling, whilst I suspect one of his nicknames, the Greyhound, must have owed something to his athleticism in the field. Nor, and rather more significantly, do I recall any colleague or opponent ever passing a negative or critical comment about him, surely extraordinary in the inevitably enclosed world of professional cricket.

At all times Brian was a pleasant, quiet and controlled man with absolutely no side to him. It must be rare for such a sporting star to keep his feet so securely on the ground.

In the years after, on my rare visits to Old Trafford, he was never any different. My last visit was 2 years ago as his guest during his Presidency of the Club. Brian had not changed.

Yet for all the memories that I have of "George's" exploits whilst playing together, perhaps the strongest personal memory is from when I was playing later as an opponent for Warwickshire against Lancashire. The match was at Coventry, Courtaulds, a smallish ground. Coventry had a reputation for helping pace and seam. As all his colleagues knew, Brian rarely used the bouncer. When asked occasionally to soften up an opponent, or to retaliate, he always replied that he hoped he was a good enough bowler to remove an opposing batsman without involving physical intimidation. At this time of my career I stood, on occasion, perhaps a yard outside of the batting crease so as to gain the initiative to attempt to upset a bowler's rhythm and length. I did this to Brian and scored a four through the covers. I was not aware that he had noticed my move, I should have seen that he looked a little strangely at me. The next ball was a bouncer, his splendid bouncer which was usually about throat level leaving you uncertain whether to play or not. Instinctively and defensively I raised my bat, fortunately the ball struck the handle in front of the throat. Brian smiled and in a quiet and measured tone said "Don't do that to me Bob!" What a splendid lesson! No need for hysteria. Just a quiet lesson in not taking advantage. A rare and very special man.

> "I was tremendously impressed last week at Lord's by the bowling and presence of Brian Statham. How he will be missed in the Lancashire team of tomorrow."
> **Neville Cardus In a letter to his friend Harold Priestley when Brian retired.**

Bob Bennett

Bob Bennett was born in Bacup and played as an amateur at Old Trafford in 1961-66 and was capped in 1963. He made 49 first-class appearances with a highest score of 112 against Nottinghamshire at Trent Bridge. He was a Member of the Lancashire 2nd XI double team which won the Minor Counties and 2nd XI Championship in 1964. Originally co-opted to Committee in March 1973 and appointed Chairman in 1987 for 11 years. He was invited by T.C.C.B. to manage England "A" teams which toured Kenya and Zimbabwe 1990, Pakistan & Sri Lanka 1991 and South Africa 1995. He was England Tour Manager to New Zealand in 1991, India 1993 and the West Indies 1998, and also for the World Cup competition. He is now a Vice President of Lancashire CCC and lives in the Isle of Man.

On the first day that the playing staff reported for the start of the 1958 season, the then Lancashire Coach, Stan Worthington, emerged from his office and entered the junior professional's room seeking out the new recruits. He escorted us up the stairs and into the 'away team' dressing room where we were lined up wondering what our mission was. The Coach then left the room to return several minutes later followed by probably Lancashire's greatest ever seam bowler. I had never seen or met Brian Statham before but I knew instantly who he was as I had read about his tremendous skill and his sub-stantial achievements. Brian at this time was only eight years into his career and had already become a legend due to his enormous talent, personality and natural modesty.

It was a meeting I will never forget and at the time, little did I know, that our paths would cross regularly for the next forty years. During all those years I never saw him raise a finger, or indeed his voice in anger. His commitment to Lancashire cricket both on and off the field was immense and I have always felt extremely proud that I had the privilege of working with him both as a player and as a member of the Committee. Many great Presidents have held office over the years and when he eventually did serve in that capacity he did so with tremendous enthusiasm, dignity, humility and sincerity.

At the start of a new season in the early sixties Brian had not been on tour that previous winter and had spent the time, with slippers on, completely relaxing. He didn't come to the indoor sessions during the first two months of the year and he didn't turn up on the morning we reported for the new season and outdoor practice in March. Several days into the early outdoor nets I padded up and entered the first in a line of nets. I took guard, played reasonably for a time and then in the distance out from the tunnel under the ladies stand, I spotted Brian walking purposefully towards the net area, sweater slung casually over his shoulder. Up to the box of balls, the best ones had long gone, he just took the nearest one, dropped his sweater gently to the ground and walked to net one. There was no thought of loosening up because he had actually bowled only six months earlier in the previous September, just three paces back and into the flow once again. Down it came that little grubby ball, no shine, but he didn't need that, pitched leg perfect length and then off the seam to hit off stump. *Pure Genius.*

The Northamptonshire visitors' dressing room provided another lasting memory. Brian, the quiet man who showed little emotion, was sipping his half of lager after the close of play when into the room walked the home team captain, Keith Andrew, to bid us farewell for the evening before going home. *"An interesting day's play"* he said before making a fatal mistake, by adding as he left *"The game's nicely poised".*

Keith departed and as the door closed the quiet unemotional JBS surprised us all by saying *"He'll think so at one o'clock tomorrow".* After lunch the following day we packed our bags to drive north with maximum points in the bank.

There is no doubt that Brian would have graced any era and it is still difficult to believe that such a naturally fit and talented person is no longer a part of Old Trafford. Fortunately his memory will live as long as cricket is played at the ground and probably well beyond. He was truly a fine man.

Bob Berry

Bob Berry was born in Gorton, Manchester. An orthodox left-arm slow bowler he utilised his diminutive stature (5ft 6in) to accentuate a full range of flight variations.

He made his Lancashire debut in 1948 and two years later he was awarded his county cap. His two Test appearances also came in the summer of 1950 and in the first at Old Trafford he returned match figures of nine for 116. He toured Australia with Freddie Brown's 1950-51 team.

In July 1953 Bob took all ten Worcestershire wickets for 102 runs in the match at Blackpool. After another season with Lancashire and a total of 259 first-class wickets he left to join Worcestershire. He took five for 65 on his debut against the South Africans and went on to take 250 wickets for them, before ending his first-class career with Derbyshire for whom he took 97 wickets. In a county career that finished in 1962 Bob took 703 first-class wickets, average 24.73.

I remember when Brian came for a trial at Old Trafford. The first-team and the trial-ists were split up into two teams. The umpires were Harry Makepeace and Stan Worthington and Brian in his trial match for the county got a couple of early wickets and would have got more but for the ruling that no-one could be out with an LBW deci-sion. Brian bowled me with an off-spinner and looked quite pleased with it until Harry Makepeace looked sternly at him and said, "You're on trial as a fast bowler so bowl quick!" Needless to say Brian was offered professional terms and joined Lancashire thankfully as a fast bowler not an off-spinner!

When Brian came over to Australia with Roy Tattersall on the 1950-51 tour there was much leg-pulling when they arrived because Cyril Washbrook and I said they had been sent by the Lancashire committee to keep an eye on us!

An outstanding innings from Brian Statham, who scored only five half-centuries in 647 innings, was a rare occasion. And the one to savour most came against Leicestershire at Old Trafford in 1955 when he scored 62 in 31 minutes with twelve 4s, two 6s and two singles, before taking four for 34 in the innings win. Statham recalled it as a good, old-fashioned slog. "I thought for a minute I was a batsman," he said. But Cyril wasn't too impressed. "Tell that silly young bugger to get out now," he said. "He wanted me to bowl for the last half hour."

Brian Bearshaw, Extract from 'From the Stretford End' (1990)

Joe Blackledge

Joe was born in Chorley and educated at Repton. He played for Chorley in the Northern League and when he was asked to captain Lancashire in 1962 did not have any first-class experience. In a difficult season for the county he played in 26 matches, scoring 569 runs, an average of 15.37 with a top score of 68.

At the end of the season he returned to League cricket and his business life. He served the county as a committee member for many years and was elected President of the Club for 2001-2002.

The first time I came into contact with Brian was in the early fifties. He had just come out of the League and we were playing Worcester Seconds in what was then the Minor Counties Championship at Blackpool.

We had scored 400 plus at tea on the first day and had bowled Worcester out fairly cheaply in their first innings. We laboured all the second day without much success and had got about half of them out and the game looked like petering out into a draw as Minor Counties in those days was played over two days.

The new ball was due and we took it at 5.50.pm. Half an hour later we were all having a shower, Brian having bowled them out in quick sticks. We all knew we were seeing a great fast bowler, needless to say he didn't play Second team cricket much after that, going straight into the First team and having great figures against Yorkshire in his debut season.

Many years later when I had the honour to captain the county he was a great help to me personally.

Alan Bolton

Alan Bolton was born in Darwen and made his debut for Lancashire in 1957. He played 40 matches between 1957-1961 with a highest score of 96 v Leicestershire at Leicester in 1959. When he left Lancashire he returned to play with Darwen after five seasons of county cricket.

It is very hard to find words to express thoughts about Brian who was such a great player. One word sums him up RESPECT. From all his team-mates who played alongside him as well as whose who played against him.

I remember one incident when we played Warwickshire and M J K Smith was playing for them. He was a player who always played with his front foot well down the wicket. We told Brian to bowl a bouncer at him, something unusual for Brian. MJK didn't know what had hit him!

Jack Bond

Making his Lancashire debut in 1955, he was dismissed for 0 and 1 by Lock and Laker in the match against Surrey. A few seasons later, he delighted in taking a century off both bowlers. He scored the first of 14 centuries for Lancashire in 1959 when he made 101 not out against Nottinghamshire at Trent Bridge.

In 1961 he was awarded his county cap after scoring three centuries. The fol-

lowing summer was the best of his career, as he scored 2,125 runs and a career best 157 against Hampshire at Old Trafford. He was a very good fielder and his unbelievable catch to dismiss Asif Iqbal in the 1971 Gillette Cup Final at Lord's was the one that turned the game.

Appointed captain of Lancashire in 1968, the county were Sunday League champions twice, won the Gillette Cup three times and finished third in the Championship twice. After a season as Lancashire coach he spent 1974 as Notts player-manager. He coached schoolboys and was a Test selector for one season. He was Lancashire's manager from 1980-86 and then a first class umpire. He is now retired and a Lancashire Vice-President.

I count myself very lucky and privileged to have spent most of my playing career under the influence of "George" as Brian was known.

I cannot think of a better role model for any young cricketer than Brian. He was a world class bowler and yet he never forgot the vehicle (County Cricket) that got him to the top. His physical effort was just as great for Lancashire as it was for England.

His influence helped me to keep a steady balance between success and failure, never too excited in victory, never too depressed in defeat and always aware of other people's efforts.

Brian was also as straight in everyday life as the ball he bowled.

Arthur Booth

Arthur Booth was born in Droylsden and was working as a draghtsman when he played four matches for Lancashire between 1950 and 1951. His most notable performance was an innings of 253 for Lancashire Second XI v Lincolnshire in 1950, a Minor County record. He played for Ashton-under-Lyne and Werneth in the Central Lancahire League, captaining both.

I recall on one occasion early in Brian's career when he bowled all through the first day, taking eight or nine wickets and then to our surprise went out roller skating in the evening! Second morning he bowled out the opposition yet again.

My wife, who didn't know Brian in his playing days, once remarked to Brian whilst looking up at the giant photographs over the main entrance to Old Trafford "Surely you must be a legend". His reply, with a self deprecating smile, was "Surely you mean a LEG END!"

Geoff Clayton

Born in Mossley, Geoff Clayton was a fine wicketkeeper, certainly above the average, good enough to establish his place in the Lancashire team as soon as he returned to the county as a 21 year-old in 1959 after completing his National Service. He was a more-than-capable batsman, stubborn and sound. He played 185 times for the county, scoring 4,410 runs, average 19.09 with 428 dismissals.

In 1962 he had 92 victims - a figure surpassed only by George Duckworth - and he was considered among the best wicketkeepers in England. He claimed 71 in 1963 when he also played his highest innings for Lancashire against Sussex at Hove.

When Lancashire released him in 1964 he played for Somerset for three years.

Audrey and Brian befriended me as a lad of 15, who came straight from school to Old Trafford; nothing has changed from that day or ever will.

He took me to posh diners (monkey suit), to Walton Jail or Mossley Working Men's Club - all came the same from 'a la carte' to pie and peas or potato pie.

In all the years, seven days and plenty of nights a week, never once did I hear a word of self approval. Hat tricks, bowling sides out twice in two days (hardest work of all), getting some stick on a good wicket, Test matches, the many, many scorching days, bowled most of the day, every day no matter who was captain. Please imagine Ramadhin or Malcolm Hilton on the other end who used to bowl two overs to Brian's one, the chap had only just made it down to fine leg before back again. By the time it got to around 6.45 I can hear him now "Eh, tell your mate to tie his shoe lace" or "Can't he bowl a no-ball".

As the junior in the side he appointed me to take the drinks list with strict instructions, 'number of soft drinks to be separate give to the captain Joe Blackledge. Make up number of soft drinks to pints of bitter, give list to waitress!'

By 7.30 good or bad days Tommy Greenhough and I would leave him sat with just a towel over head, pint in hand, one at his feet, fag in mouth, doubled up laughing at our antics.

Even when as President of Club, he arrived at club ground, with a crowded car park, full with guests only to find my old van in his space! Months after it cost me a Park Drive which made him cough!

I could go on forever, on and off the field, never a wrong word between us.

If they both knew how much what they said all those years ago, and Audrey still says, 'the door is always OPEN,' means to me.

Roy Collins

Roy Collins was a strongly-built and talented all-rounder, an aggressive right-handed batsman and useful off-spinner. In 1961 he was awarded his county cap and scored 858 runs (26.00) and took 52 wickets (29.73) and in his last season he had flashes of inspiration, hitting 25 sixes in the season, including seven in an innings of 69 against Hampshire at Southampton. Altogether he played 119 matches for the county, scoring 3,332 runs, average 20.44 with two centuries. He also took 159 wickets, average 30.07. He played for Cheshire until 1970 and enjoyed a varied League career with Leek, Longsight, Lowerhouse, Rochdale and Blackburn Northern.

One recollection I have about Brian was during the game against Pakistan at Old Trafford. I was fielding at first slip and caught quite a good catch diving to my left low down. Brian walked down the wicket quite calmly and without any fuss, stopped in front of me and said "Well caught, Chop Chop", he knew that I was more than pleased with the catch, I knew, that he was pleased with the ball he had just delivered resulting in the catch, no hugging and kissing in those days!

My name "Chop, Chop" was the nickname I had, we all had one in those days!

Ken Cranston

Ken played several matches for Lancashire 2nd XI in 1938 and made a name for himself in wartime cricket for the Royal Navy and Combined Services, but was made Lancashire skipper in 1947 without first-class experience. He was an immediate success in every respect and was chosen for England against South Africa within two months of his Championship debut. After two fine seasons he resigned to resume his practice as a dentist in Liverpool and, although he continued to play club cricket

for Neston, a fine natural talent was lost to the first-class game. Ken Cranston was still in dental practice in his 73rd year in 1990. He is now a Vice President of Lancashire CCC and was President in 1993/94.

Strangely enough I had not really met Brian Statham until he became a Vice-President and we were both subsequently Presidents of the Club. I soon learned what I had always imagined, that he was extremely modest about his talents and had to be encouraged to talk about his cricket feats.

He was a superb opening bowler and I have vivid memories of him bowling from the Pavilion end at Lord's, using the slope to help his natural in-swing and great accuracy, with Freddie Trueman doing the opposite thing from the Nursery end. They made life very difficult for the world's greatest opening batsmen.

It has always been my belief that, if Brian had been born a few years earlier, Lancashire could have won the County Championship in 1947 or 1948 when I was Captain.

The only time I batted against him was in a Charity Match at Aigburth several years later when his second delivery removed my off and middle stump, and there was no need to turn round and see the damage. He had at least paid me the compliment of not "giving me one to get me off the mark!"

He was a lovely man and a true Lancastrian.

Jim Cumbes

Jim, one of county cricket's greatest travellers, is possessed of a friendly, easy-going attitude and ready wit which made him one of the game's most popular players and helped him become a successful broadcaster on Midlands local radio. He was an accomplished goalkeeper with Tranmere Rovers, West Bromwich Albion and Aston Villa and then joined Warwickshire as player and commercial manager in 1982, but illness curtailed his playing days. (He also played for Surrey and Worcestershire.) After six years at Edgbaston he returned to Lancashire as marketing manager and then became Chief Executive in 1998.

Brian, who was undoubtedly Lancashire's greatest fast bowler ever, was one of my two schoolboy heroes - the other being Manchester City's goalkeeper, Bert Trautman. Brian was a gentlemen in every way and such a modest man, who I don't believe ever really knew just how great he was.

When I first played for Lancashire I was twelfth man and found myself sitting next to Brian. I remember asking him during the time he had stopped smoking if it helped his breathing when he was bowling. He replied, in his dead-pan way, "My breathing is a lot better but I can't bowl" The no-smoking phase didn't last too long! When I joined the club as a youngster in 1962, the fact that I actually on occasion shared the same dressing room as him was a dream come true and when I became Chief Executive at the club in his presidential year, that was the pinnacle.

As an opening bowler, a partnership with him and Fred Trueman from Yorkshire, became one of the most feared in world cricket. I shall forever treasure the memory of that smooth accelerating run-up and whippy action which so frequently resulted in an opening batsman losing one of his stumps in the opening overs of the game.

Tommy Dickinson

Tommy Dickinson showed such promise as a youth that an opening attack of him and Brian Statham was regarded as a likely, and exciting proposition. However he chose an academic career and eventually became a schoolmaster in Bristol, Blackpool and Taunton, during which time he was chief examiner in mathematics for the Joint Matriculation Board. He played just 4 matches for Lancashire in 1950-51 as an amateur and later played 5 times for Somerset. Originally he played for the local East Lancashire club and later for Keynsham CC and Blackpool CC.

After fifty years it is not easy for me to remember many incidents, particularly as there were very few matches that we played together. Towards the end of the 1950 season I was fortunate enough to "Bowl at the other end" in two first team matches. The first was at Bournemouth where we merely took a bit of shine off the ball before Roy Tattersall and Bob Berry got to work. The second was at the Oval - a much more important occasion - where Brian (and others) thought Lancashire had found a supporting fast bowler. Alas, this was not to be, partly because I was not prepared to chance my luck as a pro-

fessional cricketer, but more importantly because I discovered I was not fit enough (nor good enough) to bowl flat out on up to six days a week throughout the summer.

However, we did form a friendship and from afar I admired his achievements. Occasionally I met up with him again and even though he had become an established world class bowler and I had ventured into other avenues of life, he was always the same Brian Statham I had met at the start.

He may not have been the world's greatest fast bowler but he would certainly have been challenging to be considered as the world's most respected fast bowler.

Letter from Brian Statham to Tommy Dickinson March 1951 whilst on tour in New Zealand:

I couldn't get hold of any "Toe caps" for you in Australia, but I'll see what I can do here for you. We had pretty hot weather in Aussie, especially in Adelaide where we had several days over the 100 mark and that's pretty warm when you have to try to bowl a bit quick, which I didn't manage to do over there. I just couldn't get going at all. However I have just about got going now, I bowled much quicker in the last two matches, one of which was the Test against New Zealand. The wickets in Australia surprised me, they were very true of course, but rather easy paced, slow in fact, especially Adelaide, it was terribly slow. At Melbourne the wicket had a bit more life in it and it was a little quicker there, but the wickets don't give you any encouragement at all. Bob and Eric Hollies had a pretty lean time, they don't spin it much and hardly ever turned a ball out there.

The Australian people gave us a very good time while we were over there, we were never short of somewhere to go, lots of parties etc. The pubs shut at 6 p.m. over there though, here too, that is probably the reason for a lot of the parties they give for no apparent reason, bar drinking. It's murder in the pubs from 5 p.m. to 6 p.m, they fight for beer and drink as much as they possibly can in that one hour after work. Well Tom that's the lot I think. We'll be home inside a couple of weeks now. Remember me to Derek Broadbent when you see him will you Tom, I knew him pretty well at school. I hope you are doing okay with the saving. Keep fit, there are only the two of us to do the seam bowling next year as far as I know. It's okay bowling with you at the other end I get a bit of a breather in between overs. It's a different story with Malcolm at the other end. Be good. Brian

George Duckworth

George Duckworth was a delightful character, stocky of build, but remarkably agile and with the loudest appeal known to first-class cricket. He played 424 matches for Lancashire with 922 dismissals (a county record). He played 24 times for England.

After retirement he played for Cheshire and subsequently became a sports journalist, specialising in cricket and Rugby League. He was also a farmer, hotelier and successor to Ferguson as baggage master to England Test and Touring teams, besides managing three Commonwealth touring teams to India. He died in 1966 aged 65.

From Ted McDonald to Brian Statham - I've seen 'em all. Fast bowlers, it is said are the greatest drawing cards in cricket and in my time at Old Trafford I'd played with and against some of the fastest and best bowlers in the history of the game. My first visit to the ground as a mere youngster, with just a thought of taking up cricket as a profession, was in 1921 when I went along to watch Lancashire play the all-conquering Australians under the captaincy of the astute Warwick Armstrong.

There was Jack Gregory, a giant of a man, hurling his thunderbolts down at one end and lithe, handsome, Ted McDonald, wheeling away destruction at the other. What a contrast and what a pair of fast bowlers these two were. McDonald later came to Lancashire and I kept to him for several years without ever once losing my admiration for a cricketing artist.

In England's ranks it was my lot to keep to the fast bowling of the Nottingham "terrors," Harold Larwood and Bill Voce and, of course, there were times when I also had to stand up to the onslaught of Bill Bowes, Ken Farnes and Gubby Allen - all really fast bowlers - and in the famous "body-line" series of Tests in Australia under Douglas Jardine Larwood was really at his zenith. After the second World War it was

Australia's turn to provide the cricketing heat and as a pair Keith Miller and Ray Lindwall took a lot of beating.

In the fifties it was Trueman and Statham that the Aussies feared most and it was only when fast bowlers "hunted" in pairs that the heat was really on. How did Trueman and Statham rank with the best of my playing days? It's the jackpot question and I'm ducking it for the simple reason that comparisons between one generation and another are simply not cricket!

This tribute was written for Brian's Benefit Brochure in 1961.

left to right: S.F. Barnes, Colin Cowdrey, Fred Trueman, Jack Hobbs and Brian Statham

---

Test Match at Lord's

Bailey bowling. McLean cuts him late for one.
I walk from the Long Room into slanting sun.
Two ancients halt as Statham starts his run.
Then, elbows linked, but straight as sailors
On a tilting deck, they move. One, square-shouldered as a tailor's
Model, leans over, whispering in the other's ear:
"Go easy. Steps here. This end bowling."
Turning, I watch Barnes guide Rhodes into fresher air,
As if to continue an innings, though Rhodes may only play by ear.

Alan Ross

Farokh Engineer

Farokh was one of the most successful early overseas signings by Lancashire. He was often a match-winning batsman, especially in limited over matches, as well as a brilliant wicket-keeper. He played 46 Tests for India scoring 2,611 runs with 82 dismissals including scoring 94* before lunch against the West Indies. He played 175 first-class matches for Lancashire between 1968 and 1976 and was instrumental in the county's One-Day successes in the early 1970's. He became an adopted Lancastrian and still follows the county enthusiastically as well as commentating on matches usually involving India.

In 1966 I was priviliged to have been offered contracts by four counties; Worcestershire, Hampshire, Somerset and of course Lancashire. It didn't take me very long to decide which county I would choose to sign for! Apart from hearing and reading tales about the warmth of Lancashire folk, coupled with the knowledge and wholehearted and totally biased support of Lancashire fans. I would honestly say one of the most decisive factors was the fact that I would have the opportunity to demonstrate my skills from behind the timbers to the bowling of the great J.B. Satham whom I had learned to respect and admire as a kid in Bombay, especially in harness with another great bowler and his sparring partner Freddie Trueman.

In fact in 1966 I was so overawed by opening the innings against Brian, in a Lancashire v India match at Southport that I somehow kept on whacking perfectly good and accurate deliveries from the great man to the short mid-wicket boundary and the rail-

way tracks. I am sure the great man must surely have mused to himself that any of those perfectly straight and accurate deliveries were capable of shattering my middle stump, but I must surely been on my prayer mat longer than usual that morning and only because 'Lady Luck' smiled on me that I was able to somehow despatch those fiery deliveries right across the line to the mid-wicket regions. Any other quickie(And my good mate Fred would certainly vouch for that) would almost without question have called me all the names under the sun(Lillee and Thomson included). Names that surely could not be put into print.........but instead the great Brian Statham actually complimented me on my innings. Although I did know in my heart that I was merely lucky that day and said so as we shared a beer or two after the game.

That was only the start of my long association with this great man as we travelled together to most away fixtures in my first season with Lancashire. We used to stop off at some of the most obscure pubs as we avoided motorways and it was a great honour for me to share his experiences and humility.

In spite of some of the latish nights, when the drive from down south to Manchester via one or two diversions I am pleased to recall that the next morning when the opposition was put in all the too familiar newsprint of 'caught Engineer bowled Statham' was as prominent as ever. I am also pleased to recall that on the odd occasion it was even 'stumped Engineer bowled Statham', which many a fast bowler would take umbrage to, for the 'keeper standing up ' occasionally when the situation demands. But George being George took it in his stride and even encouraged me to do so as he knew I had the confidence and his backing to do so, which certainly got so many batsmen playing off the back foot when they should have been on the front foot. Paying the price of getting themselves out LBW especially with George's lethal 'in-duckers' at great speed.

My good friend George and I, along with Audrey have had some good times from Barbados to Calcutta (just a year or so ago) where I always thought I was 'God' till I was put in the shade by the presence of the great man himself.....even by the ladies of Calcutta....Thank heavens our Audrey was by his side.....which only just gave me the edge(smile).

How we all dearly love and miss Brian...He truly never knew how very great he really was....not only as one of the greatest ever quickies but for me one of the greatest of all men.

Geoff Edrich

One of four first-class cricketing brothers, Geoff Edrich played for Norfolk prior to the Second World War, impressing with his attractive stroke-play and close to the wicket fielding. During the hostilities he was taken Prisoner-of-war and when he was freed in August 1945 he weighed just six and a half stones. The following year, both Geoff and his brother Eric signed for Lancashire.

Geoff played for Lancashire until 1958, scoring 14,730 runs at 34.74 with a top score of 167 against Nottinghamshire at Trent Bridge in 1954. He also topped 1,000 runs a season on eight occasions, with a best of 1,977 in 1952. In 1953-54 he toured India with the Commonwealth team.

In 1956 he was given the opportunity of captaining the county and of the ten matches in which he led the side, six were won. One of them being the match in which Lancashire defeated Leicestershire at Old Trafford without losing a wicket. He left the county in 1958 to play Minor Counties cricket for Cumberland and coach schoolchildren. In 2001 he was elected a Vice-President of Lancashire.

The first time I met Brian was at the start of the 1950 season. He was a slim twenty year old in uniform. All the older players had the feeling that Brian would not be strong enough to stand the stress of being a fast bowler day in day out.

How wrong we were, with his wonderful rhythmic loose action he could bowl quite long spells. Brian played a few second team games before joining us. At Bath against Somerset in July his figures were 5 for 18 off 15 overs. In his first Roses match in August in front of a capacity crowd he bowled Frank Lowson in his first over and then quickly dismissed J V Wilson and Ted Lester.

At the end of the season Brian and Roy Tattersall flew out to Australia to strengthen the England squad. He was on his way to many Test match successes.

In 1956 when I skippered Lancs, in the absence of Cyril Washbrook, Brian got 4 for 32 and 3 for 36 against Leicestershire at Old Trafford. This was the match we won without losing a wicket.

I feel very honoured and privileged to have played in the same team as Brian. He was a great fast bowler and pal.

Harry Farrar

Harry was born in Radcliffe and attended Stand Grammar School. He played in just one match for Lancashire as an amateur against Scotland in 1955 as a left-arm fast-medium bowler. He played League Cricket for Little Lever, Stand and Westhoughton.

I was selected to play in the first match of the 1955 season against Scotland as a trialist with the full senior side excepting Brian, who had just returned from Australia with the England side. Cyril Washbrook had just gone out to inspect the wicket which was green and damp looking. I was suitably overawed by the occasion. Suddenly "George", tanned and fit, came into the dressing room and was warmly welcomed. "Keen to play?" somebody enquired. "If you think I'm going to skid around on my backside out there, you'll have to think again!" was the reply. A lovely down-beat comment from a wonderful cricketer and human being.

Tommy Greenhough

Tommy Greenhough was a very talented right-arm leg-break and googly bowler with a bounding run who spun the ball sharply. Cradling the ball during a long, prancing run, he could spin it sharply and took 100 wickets in a season twice. He took 707 wickets for Lancashire, average 21.98. He played in Four Tests, taking 5-35 v India at Lord's.

He was a fairly inept tail-end batsman who once surprised himself (and Gloucestershire's bowlers) by scoring 76*. Slightly accident prone, he was susceptible to hand injuries and once fractured both ankles when he fell off a ladder. He played league cricket for Werneth.

I first came across Brian as far back as 1949. He was playing for Denton West in the North Western League and they came to Fieldhouse, a Rochdale club, which I played for.

The match to me is unforgettable, ending in a tie, 99 runs each. Brian was not as quick then as he later became, but believe me, plenty quick enough! He was a truly great bowler and in my opinion, day in and day out he was the best. His consistency was unbelievable, no doubt most cricketers will think the same. He will be sadly missed by all who knew him and cricket fans the world over.

David Green

David was released by Lancashire in 1967 and Gloucestershire made a timely capture. He was an opening bat with a cavalier approach. The shine of the new ball never noticeably bothered him and he aimed to win the psychological battle with the bowlers from the first over. His departure from Lancashire was a surprise to outsiders; after all he had made 1,000 runs for them in his first season and was vice-captain by the mid 60s. From days at Manchester Grammar School and Oxford, his batting promise was an exciting talking point. Some argued that he was just as good at rugby. There were many notable, crisp-scoring innings for Gloucestershire including a brilliant 233 in an opening stand with Milton (122) after Sussex had put them in at Hove in 1968. He scores 2,037 runs for Lancashire in 1965 and 2,137 for Gloucestershire in 1968, the latter performance earning him a place among Wisden's Five Cricketers of the Year. He now writes for The Daily Telegraph and The Cricketer.

Brian Statham always "George" to team mates and opponents, played first-class cricket for 19 seasons, a long time for a bowler of his pace.

His nickname came about because some Lancashire players viewed the presence of George Duckworth in the championship-winning sides of 1926, 1927 and 1928 as a talisman, feeling that success would not return until they had another George in the side. Winston Place volunteered for the name and when he retired Statham took it up. Since no-one could follow him, the "George" tradition lapsed.

Unlike many fast bowlers he remained highly effective right to the end of his career. In 1968, his last season, he was 38. He actually retired at the end of July, by arrangement with Lancashire, to take up a business appointment. At that time he had taken 67 wickets at 17 runs apiece and had he completed the season would surely have taken 100 wickets for the 14th time.

His 1,691 Championship wickets cost only 15.13 each, an economy rate excelled by very few bowlers of any type in the county game in the 20th century and equalled by none of his pace. He was a top-class outfielder, quick over the ground with sure hands and a powerful, unerring throw.

I cannot think what the modern fitness trainers would have made of George. They would have been happy enough that he was like whipcord, lean and loose-limbed and possessed of stamina that belied his comparatively slight physique. They would, though, have been startled at the amount of solid English food he put away - he loved his steak and chips - and they would have been shaken by his liking for a surprising amount of bitter beer, not infrequently followed by a gin and tonic or two.

As a bowler his accuracy was legendary. He was truly fast until around 1959 or 1960 and remained sharp enough thereafter. I once asked Roy Marshall, long after he had retired, whether he had looked to drive Statham. "No," replied that most destructive of batsmen, adding, "There wasn't time." However, perhaps because Statham never indulged in spectacular fusillades of bouncers, his pace was not always appreciated from the perimeter.

George was greatly disconcerted on those very rare occasions when the ball swung for him, one of which was at Buxton against Derbyshire in 1965. Boggy run-ups caused him to cut down his approach from his customary thirteen running strides to eight or nine. Bowling rather tentatively at something below fast-medium, he started the ball on his normal strict off-stump line, only to find that banana-like movement away from the bat resulted in several near-wides, an unheard of thing for him. At the end of his second over the ashen-faced George said despairingly, "I don't know what's going on." However, as the ball picked up a light coating of mud, movement through the air diminished, then eased, to the huge relief of George, whose figures for that innings were 18.5-9-16-6.

Unlike some England quick bowlers he never "saved himself" in the county game preceding a Test match, nor "took it easy" in the game that followed. He felt that his club and his playing colleagues were entitled to his best at all times and he gave it, unstintingly.

His great stature as a cricketer never distanced him from less gifted players. He was easy-going (except when the ball was in his hand), always approachable and had a lovely, dry sense of humour. Because he was chivalrous as well as tough and because he was highly competitive but entirely without rancour he was something more than a great cricketer: he adorned the game as few men have done.

Peter Greenwood

Peter was a sound batsman and off-spin bowler. His cricket, like his football was founded more on fighting spirit and honest effort than brilliance and ebullience. He was capped by Lancashire in 1949 after taking 75 wickets. Between 1948-52 he played 75 matches for Lancashire, taking 208 wickets, average 24.47 and scoring 1,270 runs, average 16.49, with one century.

He played soccer for Chester City as a wing half/inside forward. He also played league cricket for Bradshaw, Heaton, West Bromwich Dartmouth, Todmorden and Kendal.

If my memory serves me correctly, I played in the game Lancashire Seconds versus Cheshire at Oxton, 31st May 1950 when Brian began his career. He took 4-35 and 3-48 in the match.

His cricketing abilities and strength of performance on the field are well known. Off the field in the dressing room it was a pleasure to be in his company, as it was meeting up again at the Lancashire Old Players' Days to renew our acquaintance.

Ken Grieves

Ken Grieves came to England from Australia in 1947 to play soccer as goalkeeper for Bury and League cricket for Rawtenstall. He joined Lancashire in 1949, became the fourth player to exceed 1,000 runs in his debut season for the county, and eventually achieved almost every honour the county club could bestow, although he was unfortunate that his two years as captain coincided with unrest behind the scenes.

A magnificent slip fielder, he holds the Lancashire record for catches in a match (8). He took 63 catches in 1950; 54 in 1953. In all he took 555 catches for Lancashire, a career record for the county.

Subsequently he returned to League cricket, playing for Accrington, Stockport and Milnrow. After leaving Bury FC he played for Bolton Wanderers and Stockport County. He later went on to serve on the Lancashire committee before being elected a Vice-President. He died in 1992.

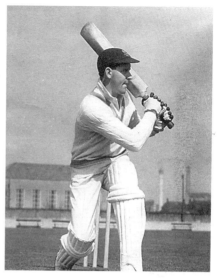

It fell to my lot in 1961 to assume the responsibility of senior professional in the Lancashire side and it was a challenge I hoped to accept and perform with satisfaction all round. For an Australian to be asked to become the skipper's "right hand man" was something new in the annals of Lancashire cricket, but I knew I could count upon the full support of all my colleagues.

None was more reliable that Brian Statham. "George" as we all called him in the dressing-room, seldom had much to say,' but when he did give vent to an opinion or volunteered some advice, whatever he had to say could be guaranteed. It would be for the good of the side in particular and for the benefit of cricket generally.

It was Brian's Benefit year and all Lancashire players were doing their utmost to make it a bumper one for him. Now that Alan Wharton had left Old Trafford I was the sole remaining player who saw Brian come into the side as a new boy. He had little to say except to seek advice and follow it. How well he benefited from what he was told was a matter of cricketing history for few players have crowded so much into so short a space of time.

In ten years Brian Statham had played and succeeded in every cricketing country of the world. England never had a more willing worker. But it is for Lancashire that Brian had bowled his heart out. Day in and day out he had spearheaded the attack with never a grouse, never a complaint and certainly never a regret. I am honoured to have called him a colleague.

**This tribute was written by Ken Grieves
in Brian's Benefit Year in 1961**

Bill Heys

Bill Heys was born in Oswaldtwistle along with Eddie Paynter. He was a baker before being signed by Lancashire as a wicket-keeper in 1957. He was one of five keepers on the staff so had limited opportunities. He played five matches for Lancashire and scored 46 against West Indies at Old Trafford in 1957. He played for Church cricket club in the Lancashire League for over 20 years.

Brian was a man who knew where the ball was going. On making my debut at Worcestershire, walking onto the field, Brian tapped me on the shoulder and said "When I go wide of the crease don't p*** off down the leg side as the ball won't be going there." As you know wicket-keepers have to read body language to be in the right position at the right time. My first victim in county cricket Don Kenyon Ct. HEYS B. STATHAM just in front of first slip "Point proved!"

Ken Higgs

Ken was a tall (6ft) robust right-arm fast-medium bowler who gave yeoman service to Lancashire and England. He generated violent momentum from a compact, bustling approach and hit the pitch so forcefully that he would jar batsmen's hands more painfully than bowlers who were quicker through the air. He took 1,033 wickets for Lancashire during 1958-1969, average 22.90. He celebrated his first appearance for England with 8 wickets against South Africa in 1965 and was the only player to appear in all five Tests against the 1966 West Indians. A resolute left-handed lower-order batsman, his simple technique, based on pushing forward with a straight bat, was rewarded with shares in two record last-wicket partnerships. Tempted out of early retirement he produced some fine performances at medium pace for Leicestershire whom he captained in 1979. When he was their coach he reappeared in an emergency in 1986 and gave his students an object lesson by taking 5 for 22 against Yorkshire. He played soccer at half-back for Port Vale.

It has been a great pleasure and privilege to have called Brian a really great friend and colleague.

In 1958 I was so thrilled and honoured to play for Lancashire County Cricket Club, my first game was against Hampshire. I was so proud, more than I could ever have imagined. Here I was actually opening the bowling with, whom I thought, one of the greatest bowlers ever. I could not help but learn from him by watching him bowl day in and day out. The proof was in the pudding when I got selected to play my first game for England at The Oval. Brian was also playing, so I played my first county and England match with my mentor - what a great honour.

I will always remember Brian as a great friend and a brilliant team mate who would listen to you and help you out if you needed anything. Goodbye Brian, you will never be forgotten.

Tyson was the fastest, but Brian Statham of Lancashire and England was the most accurate. He rarely pitched short, preferring to concentrate on line and length, gaining movement off the wicket to make the batsman play at every delivery. You ignored a ball from Brian at your peril. Only occasionally would he slip in a bouncer, disguising it so cleverly that it brought him many wickets. Its trajectory would threaten the Adam's apple rather than the skull. It skimmed off the wicket.

Extract from 'Cricket and All That' by Denis Compton. Pelham Books 1978.

Colin Hilton

Colin Hilton, well-built, cheerful and a fast bowler played 91 matches for Lancashire between 1957-1963. In 1962 he took 94 wickets, average 26.62 and altogether took 263 wickets, average 26.76. He was capped in 1962. He played 24 matches for Essex in 1964. He played league cricket for Ribblesdale Wanderers, Oldham, Morecambe, Daisy Hill and Atherton. He became the first bowler to reach 100 wickets and take 10 wickets in an innings in the Northern League.

Having known Brian for a number of years, I found him a man of two sides. On the field he would give 100% no matter what the condition of the wicket; if a batsman would play and miss or the umpire gave a decision which was half and half, he would not come out with a load of verbal (as today's players). He would turn round and just carry on doing what he was paid for.

Then there was the other side, he was a person who would do anything for you if he possibly could. I remember meeting up with him at a former players' evening, I just asked him if he would be interested in coming to my local club and we would call it, "A night with J B Statham." His answer, "Why not, what time and date". When he arrived well before time he also brought with him almost a full Lancashire first eleven. Brian grinned, "I thought it would be fun with a few more of your old pals". What a night we had, the members still talk about it to this day.

Thanks for the memory Brian, it has been an honour and a privilege to have played and known you.

My Idea of the Perfect Bowler: Brian Statham.

A captain's dream who would bowl at any end, any time and in any conditions, always putting the team first. He never argued with umpires, the opposition, the crowd or colleagues who may have dropped catches off his bowling. He was a wonderful servant to Lancashire and England and always represented cricket with dignity.

Lord Colin Cowdrey, Kent & England.

Barry Howard

Barry Howard was a batsman of style and ability. The son of Rupert Howard and brother of Nigel , he played 32 matches for Lancashire between 1947-1951. He scored 996 runs, average 23.71 with two centuries. He also played for Manchester University, Stockport, Sale and Brooklands. He was President of Lancashire CCC in 1987-88.

In the early summer of 1949 I collected an 18 year old youth at Altrincham railway station (I was 23!). The youth was Brian Statham on weekend leave from National Service. We went to play for Stockport in the Central Lancashire League. I was very impressed by his pace and accuracy. On the way home after the game, Brian told me that tennis was his real game.

Fortunately this didn't happen and in 1950 Brian was on the staff at Old Trafford and I had the great joy of Brian being my opening bowler for the Second XI.

I only had Brian for five games. In the last four he took 25 wickets at an average of 12. Strike rate 1 in 30 balls. I told brother Nigel that Brian was well ready for the First team and from then on we all know the rest.

I did not guess then that nearly 50 years later Brian would be President of Lancashire County Cricket Club. What a superb job he made of that honour.

Ken Howard

A left-handed batsman and off-break bowler, Ken played 61 matches for Lancashire between 1960-1966. He took 4-9 on his debut and in his career took 104 wickets, average 30-52. He played League cricket for Longsight.

As a boy way back in the fifties whenever we played cricket, be it at school, in the park or in the street, all the batsmen wanted to be Cyril Washbrook and all the bowlers, Brian Statham. They were every schoolboys' idols, particularly in the Manchester area.

Then in 1958 I was lucky enough to be offered a place on the staff at Lancashire. On my first day I was trembling, as you can imagine, and the first senior player to welcome me was Brian, then at lunch I was sat next to him. After half an hour talking to him I felt as though I had been a friend of his all my life.

I shall always remember Brian as being a bowler, the likes of which may never be seen again. Consistency and accuracy were second nature to him. His sportsmanship was impeccable, he never grumbled when decisions went against him, he would just turn round and get on with the next ball. Not only was he a great bowler, but he was also a brilliant outfielder. I can never recall him putting a catch down; this aspect of his game is rarely mentioned.

· Off the field he was a quiet and modest man, always having time to offer advice and encouragement, particularly to the younger members of the team.

Brian will go down in sporting history as being one of the great bowlers of all time, but in my book he was the greatest. As a player I was honoured and privileged to have played alongside him.

David Hughes

Initially a left-arm spinner and late order bat, persuaded by the limited-overs game to compromise flight and spin for flatness and economy, he became a hitter capable of such memorable performances as the late-evening destruction of Gloucestershire in the 1971 Gillette Semi-Final. As his bowling slipped away, Hughes became a high-order batsman, capable of a season's average of near 50, and finally, in his 40s he was plucked from the shadows to lead the county's match back to respectability. He played 428 first-class matches for Lancashire, scoring 10,000 runs and taking over 650 wickets. He also played in over 400 one-day matches, scoring almost 5,000 runs and taking more than 300 wickets. His former club was Newton-le-Willows CC.

Brian was one of my schoolboy heroes along with Pullar, Trueman, Dexter, Cowdrey, May, Barrington and Graveney. I was all of these in the street at home!

Brian was Club captain when I joined the staff at Old Trafford in 1967, although I never played in one of his teams, I made my debut that year against Oxford University, Jack Bond was stand-in captain. I fell over delivering my first ball in first-class cricket as I understand Brian did too, there I think the similarity ended!

In 1967 the practise nets were sighted where the office blocks are now, of which one bears Brian's name. No modern training techniques then, just cricket. I couldn't envisage Statham and Higgs going through all that. Fred Trueman keeps telling us he never bowled a straight ball, but my recollections that morning off two paces neither did Brian.

My first visit to Lord's in '68, Jack Bond set Middlesex a target of some 260, we were struggling, they seemed to be coasting at 100 for 3. Brian had already bowled quite a few overs in the match. He always seemed to look pale and drawn and Bondie asked him for one last big effort. How I got into second slip I don't know, thank God one didn't come my way! "George" bowling from the Pavilion end brought one down the hill to bowl Titmus. Next over a leg cutter up the hill to have Mike Smith caught behind by "Rookie" and next ball had John Murray leg before shuffling across. Harry Latchman also went LBW and Middlesex were 120 odd for 7, incredible! At the end of '68 both Statham and Pullar had left Lancashire, but I had played with my heroes! Just around the corner was the start of five great years for Lancashire under Jack Bond.

> Of England's fast bowlers since the war, Tyson, for a short time, was the fastest, Statham the most accurate and Trueman the most volatile.
>
> **John Woodcock, Cricket Correspondent, The Times**

Jack Jordan

A lower order, right-handed batsman and a useful wicket-keeper, Jack played 62 matches for Lancashire between 1955-57 with 128 dismissals. He was capped in 1956 after taking 56 catches and 7 stumpings during the season. He played Club cricket for Rawtenstall and Burnley.

Playing with Brian you soon realised that beneath that modest and unassuming nature was a steely resolve to get rid of batsmen as soon as possible.

Keeping wicket to him was made as easy as it ever could be because of his legendary accuracy. A brilliant talent. A tragic loss.

Peter Lee

Peter Lee signed from Northamptonshire as support to Lever and Shuttleworth, was so successful that he soon became Lancashire's number one bowler. In 1973 he became the first Lancashire bowler to reach one hundred wickets since Ken Higgs in 1968. His 101 wickets, 144 in all competitions made him the leading wicket-taker in the Championship.

In 1975 he took 112 Championship wickets at 18.45 runs each, a superb achievement with a best of seven for 8 against Warwickshire at Edgbaston. The following season he took 66 wickets, the only Lancashire bowler to exceed fifty wickets.

Peter continued to play for the county until 1982, finishing his career with 496 wickets at 23.82 runs each and a best of eight for 34 against Sussex at Hove in 1973.

I never played with Brian but met him on numerous occasions. I found him a very friendly and genuine person, always willing to have a chat.

When I first arrived at Old Trafford I made a special point of speaking to him to ask for any advice he could give me on the art of bowling, but I was very surprised by his answer. He said "Well, I never knew which way it was going so what chance did the batsman have", but he did follow this with "Stay focused and remember above all, bowl

straight, my principle was you miss - I hit" I found this a very good principle to follow.
Once again I must say that I found Brian a very nice man and was very saddened by
his death.

David Lloyd

David Lloyd joined Lancashire in 1965 as a highly promising left-arm spinner.

In 1968 he opened the innings with Barry Wood in what proved to be a very effective move, although he did take seven for 38 against Gloucestershire at Lydney in his early years.

During the summer of 1972 Lloyd hit six centuries and, with Wood, shared in a first wicket stand of 299 against Leicestershire. In 1973 Lloyd replaced Bond as captain and was chosen to lead Young England.

He played in nine Tests for England. After scoring 46 at Lord's he hit a magnificent 214 not out against India at Edgbaston. Also in that 1974 season Lloyd captained the county unbeaten through the County Championship though they only finished in eighth position.

In 1975 he led Lancashire to victory in the Gillette Cup Final. He played 378 matches for Lancashire, scoring 17,877 runs, average 33.41 with 37 centuries.

Affectionately known as 'Bumble' he joined the first-class umpires list, played for Cumberland and was Development Officer for Kwik Cricket before joining Lancashire to coach in 1992.

He went on to coach England for three years before becoming a commentator on radio/TV.

It is very important for young players making their way in cricket to have role models and examples to look up to. I was fortunate when I was making a very unsteady start at Lancashire County Cricket Club that Brian Statham was captain and had stepped into the position at a turbulent time in the club's history.

No funny stories from me. Suffice to say that his stature at the club was massive, he was quite exemplary and could he bowl! What sort of pace? is a question regularly asked. Well, modern day I would say Glen McGrath of Australia. It is no coincidence that McGrath is probably the best in the world. He has the same attributes as Brian; terrific stamina, a repeating action and deadly accurate.

Brian was quiet and thoughtful. Many of us were privileged to be on the same field. I, for one, count myself very lucky in retaining such an insatiable appetite for the game having been influenced by him and later by Jack Bond. Yes he was a "Great" and he was a legend

Freddie Moore

Freddie, who played for Rochdale, Horwich, Elland and Walkden, was one of those bowlers whom it was hoped would make a partner to Brian Statham. However, despite some good performances, he only played 24 times for the county, taking 54 wickets including the hat-trick v Essex.

My main claim to fame was standing in for Brian whilst he played against the Australians in England. We had a good county record during that time, played ten won six.

The rare times I did play with Brian were very special to me, he never lost his temper, he was always interested in your performance and always gave 100% for the county in spite of his draining Test performances. He was also a great team man.

My Childhood Bowling Hero

Brian Statham, was a wonderfully accurate, undemonstrative and totally dedicated bowler. He had marvellous partnerships for England with Frank Tyson and Fred Trueman and was always prepared to bowl himself into the ground for his captain and his team.

Bob Willis, Surrey and Warwickshire, The Book of Cricket Lists

---

Harry Pilling

At 5ft 2ins Harry was one of the smallest of all first-class cricketers, but he was a brave and remarkably consistent number three batsman who, with better luck, may have played for England. He played League cricket for Oldham and Radcliffe. He scored 25 centuries for Lancashire. In 1976 he topped the county batting averages with 1,569 runs at an average of 52.30 and received wide support for a place in the England side to face the West Indies. A superb fielder, Harry played his last game in 1980 after scoring 14,841 runs at an average of 32.26.

My great friend and colleague Brian Statham was affectionately known as "George" In all my career I have never seen a bowler who hit the seam so consistently and bowled as straight, ball after ball, over after over, as George. His theory was that if he bowled at the wickets and the batsmen missed then he would hit.

I once asked him how he held the ball when he bowled and he told me he just put it

in his hand and bowled. He said if he didn't know which way it went, the batsman did-n't either! He was an incredibly fit man and yet his pre season training did not consist of doing press ups and sit ups like the rest of us, but going into the nets for a couple of hours with a dozen balls bowling at one stump.

In theory his bowling action was all against the coaching manuals, but when he let go of the ball he had this amazing gift of hitting the seam.

He was a very gentle man who hated hurting batsmen, relying on brain and not brawn to get his wickets. I remember playing a game against Northamptonshire on a terrible wicket at Rushden. One of their batsmen, Albert Lightfoot, had this theory against George that if the ball pitched low, in another area you played high. Unfortunately he played one ball low when he should have played high. It pinned Albert at the end of his considerable sized nose and knocked him through all three stumps. Although we were all upset it affected George the most.

It was a great pleasure to have had the chance to play with this great, great player and gentleman of the game. A well deserved legend, not only in England, but world-wide.

Winston Place

Winston overcame the loss of six vital summers to the Second World War to emerge from the conflict as the ideal opening partner for Cyril Washbrook. Tallish (5ft 11ins) and trimly built, he was a steady, reliable batsman with a sound technique who played the turning ball as well as he handled the new one. He combined application with a good sense of stroke selection and could offer the bonus of being a very safe fielder. His magnificent form of 1947 earned him a berth on the MCC tour of the Caribbean, where, after failing in his five attempts for England, he scored a century in the final innings of the series, 107 at Kingston. He scored 1,000 runs in each of the eight seasons after the war, ending his career in 1955 with 14,605 runs at an average of 36.69. He spent some time as a first-class umpire and now is a Lancashire Vice-President.

I can remember seeing Brian sat alone on a form in the dressing room. It was June 17th 1950 at Old Trafford in the county championship match against Kent. It was to be his first match for Lancashire and one of our players had heard of him and said he would become our best fast bowler for years. He took his first wicket, Arthur Fagg in the match. He also took over my nick-name of George in the dressing room.

"George" was almost self-effacing, a player's player who accepted the extremes of fate without a boast or word of complaint. He never gave a thought of a bouncer to a tailender, and even his approach to the wicket was silent. Statham became inured to his fate of beating the bat without getting a touch or missing the stumps by a coat of paint.

Extract from Alec Bedser's 'Cricket Choice', Pelham Books 1981

Geoff Pullar

Geoff was a tall left-handed batsman with a distinguished Test career. In his early years he was a middle-order batsman who was renowned as a stroke player. In 1959 he was selected to play as an opener for England because of his temperament and sound defensive technique. In his second Test match against India he became the first Lancashire cricketer to score a Test century at Old Trafford. He played in 28 Tests, scoring 1,974 runs, average 43.86, with four centuries. He made a career best 175 against South Africa at The Oval in 1960, sharing in a first wicket partnership of 290 with Colin Cowdrey. He played in 312 matches for Lancashire, scoring 16,583 runs with 32 centuries. A knee injury ended his Test career and "Noddy", as he was affectionately known, moved to Gloucestershire for two years in 1969.

Brian was best man at my first wedding and I am Godfather to Anne. He was a super man to play with, so calm, such a great trier, an attribute not often mentioned about him.

I think he was basically lazy, he used to say that no way was he sprinting 30 yards then putting all the effort into the delivery to see a batsman shoulder it away. He would say that was a sheer waste of energy.

I think he would have been an even greater fast bowler if he had had the devil of say, Fred Trueman. We had to implore him to bowl a bouncer at certain batsmen as we knew he didn't like bouncers. We would say to him "They bowl them at us, why can't they have them back". He bowled such a good bouncer, it would skim the batsman's throat, not bounce over his head, he usually got a wicket with it. He didn't like bowling bouncers because he once told me that if he hit someone he was physically sick himself.

I only saw him lose his temper twice in the 16 years I played with him and it was in a Test match at Sabina Park, Jamaica and against Transvaal at the Wanderers Club,

Johannesburg, both times the batsmen had cheated us. The first one was Easton McMorris who was caught off his glove but said it hit his arm, I was only 3 yards away at silly mid-on and I saw everything. Brian, for the first time I had ever seen him, was livid, he bowled a bouncer at McMorris which hit him on the chest. McMorris started to spit blood, you can imagine Brian's reaction, he went as white as a sheet, saying "God, I've killed him".

The only other time he lost his temper was at John Fellows-Smith who got an inside edge on to his knee and was caught and bowled, he stood there saying he hadn't hit it and the umpire gave him not out. Brian again was livid, next over he bowled a bouncer at Pom-Pom, before he'd really moved the ball (it really was quick), flipped the peak of his cap and knocked it off. The next ball you could have driven a bus between Fellows-Smith and the leg stump, sure enough out flew the middle.

These were the only times I ever saw Brian lose his temper.

I shall miss him very much indeed, he was a big part of my life for nearly twenty years, I feel honoured to have been a friend of his.

John Roberts

John began his career as an amateur with Kearsley and went on to play twice for Lancashire. He took 119 wickets in Minor Counties and played 56 times for Lancashire County 2nd XI. He has been a professional in the Birmingham (Kidderminster), Huddersfield (Lascelles Hall), Ribblesdale (Padiham) and Bolton (Bradshaw) Leagues.

I only played in one first class match with Brian, but it was an experience which I never forgot. Brian was a modest and sincere man but as a cricketer his ability to bowl for long spells with accuracy and hostility set the standard for every young pace bowler. He ranks as one of the finest fast bowlers ever to grace first class cricket.

In the years that I knew him, I never heard one adverse word spoken about him. I feel honoured to have known him, both as a friend and fellow sportsman.

> Statham would bowl well with a tennis ball.
> **C L R James**
> **Extract from The Players as I knew them (1959)**

Sonny Ramadhin

Sonny bowled slowly with immaculate length and control, and at his peak seemed able to turn the ball either way, or not at all, with no change in action. At his best in his 20s with Alf Valentine, he formed the renowned "Spin twins" attack for West Indies. He took 92 wickets, average 22.23 in his first Lancashire season showing he was still to be respected, even if the old magic had gone. Sonny played for Lincolnshire in 1968-70 and his clubs included Crompton, Ashcombe Park, Radcliffe, Liversage, Wakefield, Delph, Nantwich, Little Lever and Daisy Hill. He still lives in Lancashire. His daughter Sharon became the wife of Willie Hogg (Lancashire and Warwickshire) and their son Kyle is now on the Lancashire staff.

I knew Brian from the early 1950s. I played a few Tests against him and I always found him to be a gentleman and one of the finest fast bowlers in the 50s and 60s. Nothing seemed to get him down, when he had decisions against him he just carried on bowling.

I played under him at Lancashire and I enjoyed my short stay playing with him. He always went out of his way to give advice and he made me very welcome at Old Trafford. I shall miss seeing him when I go there.

John Savage

John was born in Ramsbottom and as an off-spinner made his name with Leicestershire, but returned to his native county, first as a player and then, from 1970 as a respected member of the county's coaching staff. He played 281 matches for Leicestershire, taking 100 wickets in a season three times. He also played 58 matches for Lancashire between 1967 and 1969. He was elected a Vice-President of the county club in 2001.

Brian Statham was for many years a top class county and international bowler. My first encounter with him was in the early 60s at Grace Road, Leicester. Unfortunately for me, I was 22 yards away with bat in hand on a quick Grace Road wicket. Needless to say my innings didn't last too long!

I do believe that Brian took more wickets bowling against Leicestershire than he did bowling against any other individual county (one for the statisticians).

When I returned "home" back to Lancashire I played the 1967 season when Brian was captain. That season we had an extremely good pace attack led by Brian. The one outstanding performance from my point of view regarding Brian was when he played his last match before retiring in 1968 in the Roses match at Old Trafford. Yorkshire all out for 61, Brian had taken 6 wickets for 34 runs..

Brian was a gentleman on and off the field. Through my long career at Old Trafford my memory is of being good friends with both Audrey and Brian.

Ken Shuttleworth

Ken, strongly built and tall with a superb action, made his Lancashire debut in the summer of 1964 in the Roses game at Old Trafford, taking the wicket of Geoff Boycott. However, he took a while to establish himself at Old Trafford and it was 1968 before he was awarded his county cap.

His best season for the county was 1970 when he took 74 wickets at 21.60 runs apiece. That summer also saw him play for England against The Rest of the World at Lord's and at the end of the season he toured Australia with Ray Illingworth's side. He took 5 for 47 at Brisbane and played in four of the Tests. His best figures for Lancashire were 7 for 41 against Essex at Leyton but in 1975, after a career plagued with injuries, he played his last game for the county. Having taken 484 wickets at 22.92 runs each, he moved to Grace Road to end his career with Leicestershire. He is now a first-class umpire.

I feel very privileged to have known and played with Brian. He very rarely showed any emotion or anger, choosing instead to bowl the opposition out. He loved getting wickets and treasured every one, whether it be no 1 or no 11. A wicket was a wicket to Brian. He was a great bowler and undoubtedly the best there was to knock over those stubborn tail-enders.

However on one occasion I remember he was a little embarrassed by one particular wicket. We were playing Worcestershire at Old Trafford on a green wicket. We went into the game with four seamers, Brian, Ken Higgs, Peter Lever and me. We won the toss and asked Worcestershire to bat first. Statham and Higgs opened the bowling. Unbelievably, neither got a wicket in their opening spell. On came Lever and Shuttleworth who proceeded to bowl Worcestershire out, only to encounter one of those stubborn last wicket stands between, arguably the two biggest rabbits in the game at the time, Jack Flavell and Len Coldwell. Peter and I tried for a further four overs each, by which time Brian was pleading with us to finish the innings off. We failed and a reluctant Brian had to come back. He started to take his sweater off, but having got it half way, put it back on, muttering to the umpire that it wasn't worth taking off. His first ball was nicked to second slip. Duncan Worsley dived to his right, got a hand to it but palmed it about three yards away. Up he got, retrieved the ball. Flavell and Coldwell were each three yards down the pitch on a yes-no interlude, wondering whether to risk a single. Duncan was about to have a shy at the stumps to run one of them out. Suddenly a voice boomed out "Don't you dare." Duncan's face was a bemused picture. Brian added "That's a first-class wicket you're trying to run out."

Brian's second ball knocked the off stump out of the ground. It had taken him two balls to do what Peter and I had tried to do for eight overs. Our excuse was that we were tired!

He was one of the greats and a gentleman. Everyone who knew Brian will miss him

Jack Simmons MBE

Jack was appointed Chairman of Lancashire County Cricket Club in September 1997. A Lancastrian born and bred, he joined Lancashire in 1968 as a promising youngster of 27! His overall first-class record featured some 1,033 wickets and 9,417 runs with a county cap awarded in 1971 and a Benefit in 1980. He played cricket for Enfield, Baxenden, Barnoldswick and Blackpool before joining Lancashire and helping them win the John Player League titles in 1969 and 1970 and four Gillette Cup successes in 1970,71,72 and 75. In 1984 they won the Benson & Hedges Cup. Jack also helped Lancashire win the Refuge Cup and he captained Tasmania to victory in the Australian Gillette Cup in 1979. The true measure of a player is the first-class game. Here Jack has become one of Lancashire's leading all-rounders, taking over 1,000 first-class wickets and scoring over 9,000 runs. He was honoured in 1985 as one of Wisden's Cricketers of the Year and he has always been a great ambassador for Lancashire and England. The greatest honour Jack has ever received was in January 1990 when he was awarded the MBE in the New Year's Honours List.

Unfortunately I never played with Brian, making my debut in 1968 late season when Brian had already announced his retirement.

Either the following year or in 1970 I played against him for Lancashire in a Benefit game, he was guesting for a club or a Bolton league side. I was in reasonable form with the bat at the time, facing a retired Brian Statham. The ball pitched leg stump and hit off. It would have bowled Boycott never mind Jack Simmons! On my way back to the Pavilion I passed Brian and asked why was he retiring when he could still bowl balls like that. He just smiled and I carried on my way to the dressing room, quite proud that I had been bowled by a magnificent ball from one of the greatest fast bowlers ever.

He continued to have that unassuming smile and the presence

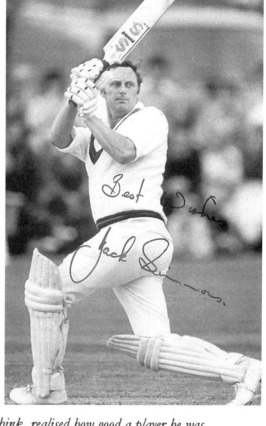

of a modest man who, I still don't think, realised how good a player he was.

When he joined the Committee and then was elected to be President in 1997/98, he always did the job to the best of his ability. Another position he held with distinction was President of Lancashire Schoolboys. I have been asked since his death to fill this position. It is an honour and gives me great pleasure to follow the great man.

He always got me out. The nicest bloke in the game.
One of the finest of all quick bowlers.

Tom Graveney

Ken Standring

Ken made a wonderful start when he dismissed Len Hutton as his first victim in first class cricket, but he subsequently found little time in the game at that level playing only 8 times for the county. At various times he played for Farnworth, Bingley, Bradshaw, Southport & Birkdale and Ribblesdale Wanderers. He was secretary to the Lancashire Cricket Federation for over 20 years, and was appointed secretary of the Lancashire Cricket Association in 1991, becoming assistant secretary of the Lancashire Cricket Board when it was established in 1996.

I only played in a limited number of games for Lancashire First XI and, indeed, Brian was not playing in all of them as he was often on duty for England.

I do remember that he was always prepared to help a young bowler whenever possible, This was illustrated during one match - I think it was against Leicestershire, but my memory may be incorrect. I was bowling and Brian was fielding at mid-off. As he returned the ball to me he said very quietly "Make sure you are well behind the crease next ball - the previous ball was a no-ball" (This hadn't been called by the umpire - Hugo Yarnold).

I did as he had said, but was disgusted when, although about a foot behind the crease, the umpire no-balled me. Evidently it was Hugo Yarnold's policy to give a no-ball next ball if he had missed one! I felt particularly sore about that policy - Two wrongs don't make a right!

I would have loved to have fielded in the slips to Brian - to see exactly what he did with the ball - but as a new boy and a medium fast bowler, I was always put down at third man or fine leg - so didn't get the close-up view I would have liked.

When I was working at Old Trafford as Secretary of the LCA and subsequently as Assistant Secretary of the LCB I was always most impressed by Brian's manner. He was always friendly, unassuming and conscientious in his duties for the county - as usual a model to everyone.

Prof Sir Colin Stansfield Smith CBE

Colin made his debut for Lancashire as an amateur in 1951 against Hampshire at Liverpool, the same match that Tommy Greenhough made his first appearance. As a right-arm fast bowler and bat, he went on to play for his county for the next six years - before a career in architecture became his priority. He played 45 matches for Lancashire in 1951-57 and was capped in 1956.

Born in Didsbury in 1932, Colin attended William Hulme Grammar School before going to Christ's College, Cambridge. He played for Cheshire whilst at school and was called up for National Service in 1950 when he played for the army.

He gained a Blue at Cambridge in each of his four years, scoring an undefeated century against Warwickshire at Edgbaston in 1957 - opening with Bob Barber and batting with Ted Dexter. He was top wicket-taker for the University in his last two years.

In 1958 he started work as an architect in Dulwich and played cricket for his town, but it was his job that demanded his time. He became one of Britain's leading architects, awarded a gold medal in 1991 and knighted two years later.

When playing for Lancashire the Committee considered him for the captaincy but he could not devote enough time to sport. He maintains a keen interest in Lancashire cricket, 48 years after his Aigburth debut.

I played with Brian (George) at the beginning of his career with Lancashire after his and during my national service and time at the University. It was a rare privilege. Brian always had a quiet reserved understated confidence. He was the opposite of the fast bowler stereotype. Instead of the macho aggressive, menacing, sledging loud mouth, Brian was the quiet, line and length, rhythmic graceful gentleman. Not that he wasn't menacing, but his armoury was the rapier rather than the broadsword. He was always the one at national level to volunteer or be presumed upon to bowl uphill against the wind. For him it did not matter because his accuracy was legendary - in his words if the batsman missed he hit from which ever end he bowled.

His action was impossible to replicate because of his double jointedness and yet the poetry of the flow and the balance of the delivery stride were always unforgettable. I am also reminded of Brian's throwing arm which was unequalled in cricket at that time and

as a fielder in the deep he had no peer.

He was so much the gentleman he hated bowling bouncers, he did not need them in his repertoire but when he did (after coercion from Cyril), his were truly deadly, inside shoulder at neck-height and batsmen were mesmerised, not knowing which way to sway. I often thought that Brian would have got even more wickets if he had allowed himself to stray from that immaculate line and length. His bowling partner would always enjoy the benefit of his sustained accuracy. His standards were so professional, always seeking to bowl the perfect ball. From the very first sighter to the last ball of every game his line and length were totally predictable.

Brian will be remembered for the standards that he set on the field, but he was always generous to any supporting cast, particularly the younger ones. His wry, dry wit invariably added to the day's entertainment. Cricket will never see his like again.

Roy Tattersall

Roy began his career with Lancashire at the age of 25 as a seam bowler. After two seasons he was persuaded to try off-spin and was an immediate success, taking 193 wickets, average 13.59, to put him at the top of the national averages. He was 6ft 3ins, slim and with a high action, his changes in flight and direction made him a difficult proposition for batsmen. He played in 16 Test matches, taking 58 wickets at an average of 26.08 with a best return of 7 for 52 against South Africa at Lord's in 1951. In 277 matches for Lancashire he took 1168 wickets, average 17.39, including 9-40 against Nottinghamshire at Old Trafford which included a hat-trick with 4 wickets in 5 balls. He was in and out of the Lancashire side at the end of the 1950s and this was a sad and unaccountable end to a most dis-

tinguished career. He was a superb bowler, courteous, always ready to help a younger player and someone who was always willing to bowl, even to the best batsmen. He is now a Lancashire Vice-President.

I first met Brian in April 1950 when he reported for a trial at Old Trafford. He impressed right away and joined the staff in May, just two weeks after leaving the RAF. He played in two or three games for the 2nd XI before his rapid promotion to the first team. His speed and accuracy, for one so slim, surprised many a batsman.

We struck up a friendship and roomed together at our away games in his first season. I was eight years older than Brian and he welcomed advice and asked many questions in his quest to succeed. It was a great season for us both, as Lancashire were joint champions with Surrey. September came and we said our farewells, thinking we would see each other next April.

Just before new year 1951, Brian and I were notified that we were to be sent to Australia to join the MCC tour party. What a thrill for both of us! Neither of us had flown before and the flight took four days in a four-engined propeller driven Constellation aircraft. We each had a bed for four hours in the Raffles Hotel in Singapore but other than that we had to sleep on the aircraft.

On meeting the other members of the MCC party in Melbourne, I had to introduce Brian to more than half of them because he had never played against them, such was his rapid success for a twenty year old. Brian did not play in the Tests in Australia but played his first Test in New Zealand at Christchurch. One short month after seeing his first Test match, he was playing in one!

Brian was now a permanent member of the Lancashire and England teams. Never boastful and always unflappable, whatever the situation he enjoyed his cricket. We had many a good laugh together at incidents that happened both on and off the field. Brian's quiet manner belied a truly entertaining personality and a most dry sense of humour.

Across his career Brian's record speaks for itself, his first class averages were; bowling - 2260 wickets at 16.36 runs each and batting - 5424 runs at 10.80 and 230 catches. In 70 Test matches he took 252 wickets at 24.82. 675 runs at 11.44 and 28 catches.

I can honestly say that I have never heard anyone say a wrong word about Brian, only praise. You could not have a better team-mate, always giving 100%, even when tired and sometimes over-bowled, he never complained. He is acknowledged the world over for his accuracy and consistency. Many is the time I heard him advise an opposition batsman to "rub it, I know it hurts" when he had hit the player in the legs.

Once his playing days were over, Brian was voted on to the Committee for many years. He then became a Vice-President and later became President of LCCC. With the support of his wife Audrey, Brian worked hard to be a most respected and popular

President. He also took a great interest in the youth cricket of Lancashire.

Brian is very much missed by his wife and family and his countless friends and not least by myself and my wife, Phyllis. Up to his death we remained firm friends, sharing many holidays and frequently staying at each others' homes and enjoying each others' company.

Brian has passed on but will never be forgotten.

Cyril Washbrook

By an standard Cyril Washbrook was an outstanding cricketer. In only his second match for Lancashire he made a brilliant 152 against Surrey. His cap set at a rakish angle, sleeves folded at the elbow, his arms swinging in military precision, Cyril marched on to the field. As a batsman he played the hook and square cut to perfection and excelled at driving the overpitched ball. He was also a superb cover point fielder. He played exactly 500 matches for Lancashire, scoring over 34,000 runs with 76 centuries in all first-class cricket. He held almost every role for Lancashire in a 60-year association as captain, manager, committee member and President. He played 37 Tests for England, scoring 2569 runs with his most famous innings, the 98 at Headingley when he was recalled at the age of 41 after a six year absence. The opening partnership of Washbrook and Hutton for

England and with Winston Place for Lancashire has become woven into the fabric of cricket history. He was awarded a CBE in 1991 by the Queen and was President of Lancashire in 1989-90. He died in 1999 aged 84.

I played with Brian from 1950 to 1959 and no captain has had a more willing bowler at his command. Never once in all the years I played with him did Brian ask for a single over more or show the slightest resentment when taken off or when asked to bowl.

He carried the Lancashire attack for years and every other Lancashire bowler ought to have been grateful for his presence in the team. Brian was responsible for much of their success. Because of his unfailing accuracy batsmen must have tried to take advantage of others. A great fast bowler who rightly deserved the praise of Lancashire supporters for the service he gave to the game and, more particularly, for the manner in which he played it!

**This tribute was written by Cyril Washbrook in
Brian's Benefit year in 1961.**

Alan Wharton

An attacking left-handed batsman and more than useful right-arm medium-pace bowler, Alan made his debut for Lancashire in 1946. In 1949 he scored four centuries and became one of only nine Lancashire league amateurs to graduate to international cricket. He made his Test debut for England against New Zealand at Headingley. Injury forced him to miss the next Test and he never played for England again.

Alan's bowling, which brought him 225 wickets for the county, was never to be underestimated and in 1951 he took 7 for 33 against Sussex at Old Trafford. He scored 2,157 runs at an average of 40.69 in 1959, including his highest score of 199 (run out) against Sussex at Hove.

A TRIBUTE TO BRIAN STATHAM

At the end of the 1960 season he ended his career with Lancashire, in which he had scored 17,921 runs at 33.55, and joined Leicestershire.

He was elected Vice-President of Lancashire CCC in 1990 and was appointed President of the Lancashire Former Players' Association in the summer of 1993 shortly before his death.

It was strange facing up to Lancashire and Brian Statham that summer (1961) and the thought occurred to me that it might have been my lot to take the first over of the new season from my old fast bowling colleague. I would have enjoyed that! At the same time I knew every run would have to be earned the hard way for there was no more accurate bowler in the game than Brian.

For the better part of 10 years I had played alongside Brian. It had been my good fortune to be in the Lancashire side when he had first bowled in county cricket. From my place in the slips I remember saying that at long last Lancashire had found the man to replace burly Dick Pollard.

Throughout the whole of his career I never saw Brian show a hint of annoyance, a touch of temper or a look of disgust. Catches were dropped off him but there were no recriminations. Just a muttered apology and a cheery "Better luck next time" in reply.

I once stood with Stan Worthington behind the bowler's arm at Blackpool's Stanley Park and in the course of his opening spell we saw Brian send down 78 deliveries. The batsmen had to play at 77 of them. That was accuracy for you!

He was a happy man in reality, placid as the day was long, mellow as they come and as witty as many a stage comedian. That's the Brian I would always remember. Then it was my lot to oppose Brian whenever Leicestershire met Lancashire and no quarter was asked or given. We chatted like old pals before the match and at the intervals during it. But when the umpire called "play" Brian was after my wicket and I was seeking runs.

I ventured to suggest that no fast bowler in history has ever been quite so dominant as Brian. Just think of it? In ten years England never dropped him and Lancashire never even thought of doing so! Well played George.

This tribute was written by Alan Wharton in Brian's benefit year 1961

No professional cricketer has been more universally respect and his nickname "George" was a fitting tribute to his gentlemanly and scrupulously fair nature.

Bill Frindall

Alan 'Ranji' Wilson

Alan was born in Newton-le-Willows and made his debut in 1948 at Old Trafford in Cyril Washbrook's famous Benefit game against the Australians. Lindwall and Miller were at their best and Bradman scored an unbeaten century in the second innings. In the first, the scoreboard read: Bradman caught Wilson bowled Roberts 28. What a victim to collect on your debut!

Another proud moment came in 1958 when Alan and Roy Tattersall put on 100 runs for the last wicket against Leicestershire at Old Trafford. Alan made his highest score of 37 not out, which raised his career batting average to almost 6. The humorous dressing room nicknamed him 'Ranji' after the great Indian batsman.

He was a very good Lancashire 'keeper who competed with many others who came and went. He claimed 346 victims in his 171 matches for the County and was a very popular team man.

After his playing days 'Ranji' became a biscuit designer, a most unusual profession, and one which won him an invitation to appear on the famous TV progamme, "What's My Line".

I first met Brian when he came for a trial to Old Trafford. He was doing his national service and was in RAF uniform. He changed at the side of me as I was already on the playing staff, such a modest man and a gentleman which never changed all his life.

I kept wicket to Brian in his first second eleven match against Cheshire, he took 7 or 8 wickets and bowled a long time. At the end of the day when asked what he would be doing after the game - "roller skating" he replied.

Brian gained his second eleven cap, was promoted to the first eleven and gained his cap and went on to tour Australia all in the one season.

Keeping wicket to Brian is something I won't forget, so accurate, he always used to say "BOWL STRAIGHT". "BOWL A LENGTH" and the batsman will get himself out.

Many a batsman padded up to let the ball go through only to find his off stump knocked out. Brian was double jointed and this gave him the ability to bowl off-cutters, he then later developed outswing. If he had taken many wickets during the day and you congratulated him, he would reply "It's been a nice sunny day, hasn't it".

I remember an incident when in the early years wicket-keeping gloves were faced with rubber. I used to put oil on the face to soften them and make them tacky. After a few balls of the over I threw the ball back to Brian, it must have been so sticky that he waved the ball to Cyril Washbrook, who was then captain, and shouted "Skipper, the ball is like a Toffee Apple!"

I don't think I ever saw Brian drop a catch in the outfield, as he raced to get under the ball (which probably earned him the nickname the "Greyhound"). He was a fine fielder and threw the ball over the stumps from way out on the boundary.

On another occasion I was batting in the nets and photographers wanted a picture of Brian bowling and knocking out a stump. "Just play inside the ball" Brian said. It only needed the one ball and out it went.

Duncan Worsley

Duncan was born in 1941 and first played for Lancashire in 1960. He was awarded his Blue at Oxford University in 1961, 1962, 1963 and 1964. He was captain of the University side in 1964. He was awarded his county cap in 1966. A sound batsman, he played 62 times for the county, scoring 2,508 runs, average 25.33 with four centuries.

I made my debut for Lancashire in September 1960 against the South African Tourists at Blackpool. Brian had just had one of his most successful seasons, having topped the national bowling averages for the second year in succession and enjoyed a terrific Test season against South Africa. Furthermore, during that series, in the Test at Nottingham, he had removed one of the South Africans, Colin Wesley, for a king pair. As Wesley came into bat at Blackpool, Brian was obviously reluctant to inflict further humiliation upon him. He therefore duly ran up and bowled a low full toss which Wesley managed to get out to first ball yet again!

In the second innings Brian insisted that he was not bowling when Wesley came in. Nevertheless, Ken Higgs removed him for another pair. To me this episode summed up

Brian the man and cricketer. He had this sublime talent which he wore very lightly and I never saw him either denigrate or undermine a fellow professional or any other person. He was at all times friendly, helpful, courteous and constructive. Above all else he rose above the politics, in-fighting, backbiting and general competitiveness inherent in a professional sporting organisation.

Roy Booth

Roy Booth spent six seasons with Yorkshire but had limited opportunities before moving to Worcestershire in 1956 to become their regular wicket-keeper. He was capped in his first season taking 62 dismissals. During Worcestershire's successful 1964 County Championship campaign he became the last wicket-keeper to take 100 dismissals in a season. When he finally retired in 1970 he was the only Worcestershire wicket-keeper to take in excess of 1000 dismissals. He was a member of the County committee for 30 years and in 1999 was elected President of the club.

I moved to Worcester in 1956 from Yorkshire and for a season stayed with Bob Berry and his wife (of course an old colleague of Brian's). We were due to start a game against Lancashire on the Saturday so on the Friday evening Bob and I went along to the Diglis Hotel for a drink with one or two of the boys. The Lancs lads were keen on a game of cards (not Cyril Washbrook, skipper), however Cyril had gone out for dinner with instructions to the team for an early night. At someone's suggestion a move was made to a bedroom for a game and Bob and I went along. Time went on and we were immersed in the card game and a kitty to play for, Cyril's words were probably forgotten until heavy footsteps were heard coming nearer along the landing. Within seconds the bed was cleared, both of cards and bodies, under the bed etc. Apart from Bob and I and the two lads who were sharing the room. A knock at the door, it opened and in walked Brian! "Good evening lads, hello Bob and Roy, having a pleasant get together?" Much relief all round and I have always thought that this nice dry sense of humour typified Brian's approach to both cricket, and I suggest, life.

Martin Horton

Martin Horton gave his county fifteen seasons sterling service until in 1966, after 376 matches, when still only 32, he became New Zealand's National Coach. An ideal county all-rounder, Martin's batting became as solid as his appearance suggested; at his best opening, he developed an array of powerful scoring strokes from a meagre backlift. He was also a steady off spinner and safe fielder whose career figures of 19,945 runs, (average 29.54), 166 catches and 825 wickets (average 26.94) scarcely reflected his valuable versatility. The highest of Martin's 23 centuries was a brilliant 233 against Somerset in 1962, the 314 added with Tom Graveney setting a then Worcestershire 3rd wicket record, while, aged 21, he achieved an analysis of 9 for 56 against the 1955 South Africans, a sensational performance which remained his best. Martin exceeded 1,000 runs eleven times, and twice performed the 'double'. His two Tests were against India in 1959; he scored 60 runs in 2 innings and took 2 wickets for 59.

Brian was a model professional and one of the unsung heroes of cricket.

In all the years I played against him and on a couple of times with him, I never once heard him swear at or "sledge" the batsmen. If you edged him through the slips or he had a catch dropped he would give a wry smile and then get ready to bowl again. I never heard a bad word said about him in all the years I knew him. He was a cricketer's cricketer.

I remember when Lancashire batted most of the first day against us, they declared and left us with about 20 minutes to bat. Don Kenyon and myself opened and Brian duly got me out for a duck. In the bar afterwards he apologised for getting me out! That of course didn't stop him trying like hell when he had the ball in his hand.

Brian was probably the most accurate fast bowler of all time. His maxim was "You miss, I hit."

Brian was a quiet, modest person, at the end of a day's play as long as he had his pint of beer he was happy. He had everyone's respect as a bowler and as a person.

Peter Walker

Peter was a very tall (6ft 4ins), extremely articulate all-rounder who since his retirement, has continued to serve Welsh cricket as well as being a writer and broadcaster. He was a world-class close catcher who would rank with the best of any generation and he fully deserved to amass the fourth highest total of catches by a fielder with an entirely post-war career. It is hard to remember any morsel escaping his long reach at short-leg and he was almost as infallible when he crossed to slip. An effective but slightly awkward right-handed batsman, originally a left-arm medium-pace swing bowler, he eventually converted to orthodox slow spin. Although he has been involved with Glamorgan's cricket and many of its other activities for more than three decades, he was born in Bristol and brought up in South Africa.

Brian "George" Statham lives on here in Cardiff. Not in a literal sense of course, but in a pair of his cricket boots!

Kevin Lyons, a former colleague of mine in the Glamorgan team of the 1960's joined the first-class umpires' list after retiring. He stood in Brian's last game for Lancashire against Yorkshire at Old Trafford in 1968 at the end of which, with a typical self deprecating gesture, Brian quietly took off his battered boots which had several thousand overs in them and put them in the dressing room waste bin. "Shan't have any need for these any more" said one of England's finest ever fast bowlers.

After the dressing room had emptied, Kevin tip toed in and retrieved the boots. They are now one of his proudest possessions. When he showed them to me a little while ago, we both handled these blanco encrusted lightweight footwear - for "George", like most professional crickets of his day had his tailor-made by a Mr Whiting, a cobbler in Northampton - with great reverence. They are a fitting legacy of a great bowler in a great era of English cricket.

Brian Statham also left an indelible mark on my life, this time in a literal sense. Playing for Glamorgan against Lancashire on a diabolical pitch at Neath in South Wales, Brian bowled a good length (was there ever anything else from him?) ball which reared up and cut back to strike me a fearful blow over the left eye.

I spent a blood-stained night in the local hospital. My first, and I might add my only visitor was Brian, full of concern and remorse, typical responses from a truly gentle man.

A TRIBUTE TO BRIAN STATHAM

I took no further part in the game but returned, sporting a horrendous black eye, for the next match against Yorkshire at St Helens. Into our dressing room, as always, stormed F S Trueman. Coming straight over to me he growled "Eh lad, I read that George blackened your eye. I'll do the same to the other later today!". It was said, I now believe, in jest, but when my turn came to bat I more than half expected a bouncer first ball. Instead it was a fast, inswinging yorker which knocked my leg stump out!

You could always trust Brian - wish I could say the same about Fred. (Only in jest Fred!)

"George" to his colleagues, had everyone in trouble except Hallam, who made 106. His 12 overs cost only 28 runs and he took five wickets into the bargain. He always bowled at the stumps, just like the great West Indian, Michael Holding. If you missed, he hit - as I proved. I could never hit him off the square. Occasionally I would edge him through the slips and I'd be so embarrassed I would apologise to him. "Don't worry about it, Dickie," he would say, "That's another four runs for you." Typical that; he was a kind man. Edge Fred through the slips and the air would be as blue as my Sunday League jacket.

Dickie Bird, Extract from 'My Autobiography' 1997, Hodder & Stroughton.

**Brian leaving the field in his final match for Lancashire,
against Yorkshire at Old Trafford in 1968**

PART THREE

Statham of England

England v. South Africa, Third Test, Old Trafford, 1951

Sir George(Gubby) Allen CBE

One of the most powerful influences on the game of cricket and a major force at Lord's for over 60 years as a high-class all-rounder, captain, selector and administrator, Sir George 'Gubby' Allen was born at Bellevue Hill, Sydney in 1902. He represented Middlesex in 146 matches from 1921 to 1950 and Cambridge University in 1922 and 1923. Representing his country in 25 Tests from 1930 to 1947/8, he toured abroad 3 times including the 1932/3 Ashes series when he refused to adopt 'bodyline' tactics. He scored 750 runs with a top score of 122 v New Zealand at Lord's in 1931 and he took 81 wickets with a best of 7 for 80 v India at The Oval in 1936. He played 265 first-class matches scoring 9,232 runs and he took 788 wickets. In 1929 at Lord's he achieved 10 for 40 (8 clean-bowled) v Lancashire. President of M.C.C. in 1963-64, the former "Q" Stand at Lord's was named after him. He was knighted for his services to cricket in 1986 and died in 1989.

It is generally recognised that cricket has known few better, bigger-hearted, and perhaps more unlucky, fast-bowlers than Brian Statham. He had led the England attack for ten years and had seldom failed to make his presence felt. If he had not actually taken wickets he had worried the batsmen so neatly that his colleagues at the other end had been able to "cash in".

There can be no better example of this than the Test series in Australia in 1954-5. Without in any way wishing to detract from Frank Tyson's great success in the series, I am convinced he owed a great deal to Brian whose persistence throughout never allowed the pressure to flag for a moment.

No one who saw it can fail to pay tribute to Brian's match-winning "marathon" in the second innings of the Lord's Test against the South Africans in 1955. It was one of the greatest pieces of sustained fast bowling of the 20th century, bowling as he did, 29 consecutive overs and taking 7-39.

Watching him on the field, his quietly cheerful expression and his lethargy until the moment demanded, radiated a delightful and modest character. As a selector for some years, I would like to pay a tribute to him for his help and friendship and for his truly great contribution to English cricket!

This article was written by Gubby Allan in Brian's Benefit year in 1961

Sir Alec Bedser CBE

Alec Bedser was a massively built right-arm fast medium bowler who was rated by Don Bradman as the most difficult bowler he faced. Representing England in 51 Tests, he took 236 wickets (average 24.89) with best figures of 14 for 99 v Australia at Trent Bridge in 1953. He toured abroad eight times. Playing 485 first-class matches, he took 1,924 wickets (average 20.41), scored 5,735 runs (average 14.51 and he held 289 catches. He later became Chairman of the England Selectors (1969 to 1981), managed two MCC tours abroad and subsequently became club President of Surrey in 1987. He was awarded the OBE in 1964, the CBE in 1982 and Knighted in 1997 for his services to cricket. He was appointed Hon. Life Vice-President of M.C.C. in 2000. He is inseparable from his twin brother Eric, who was an all-rounder (off-spinner) who contributed a great deal to the county during Surrey's seven consecutive Championships in the 1950s.

I was fortunate to be associated with Brian from the start of his career.

My first memory of Brian was in 1951. He and Roy Tattersall were flown to Australia to join the MCC team to Australia 1950/51 tour as a twenty year old. He arrived in South Australia in January 1951 looking rather pale with the temperature at 104 degrees. It was a shock to him especially as he was called to play almost immediately in that heat. He stuck it out and he proved at once what a great trier he was. Brian was a great team man and fine tourist. I never remember him ever complaining, he just got on with the job in hand. He was a great companion to travel with and especially to enjoy a few beers.

As well as being a fine bowler he was an ornament to the game, There were no histrionics from Brian, he would not have approved of some of the antics one sees today.

Trevor Bailey

Trevor Bailey, one of Essex and England's greatest all-rounders, played for the county from 1946 until 1967, being captain from 1961 to 1966. A fast scorer for Essex, he often adopted a defensive role for England. He was a fast-medium bowler with a high action and fielded brilliantly. He played 61 Tests between 1949 and 1958-59. In first-class cricket he scored over 28,000 runs and took over 2,000 wickets and did the "Double" 8 times, scoring 2,000 runs and taking 100 wickets in 1959. He won Blues at Cambridge for cricket and football and won an FA Amateur Cup winners medal with Walthamstow Avenue. Since retiring he has written many books, worked for over 30 years on "Test Match Special" and was cricket and football correspondent of the Financial Times for 20 years.

I never encountered a cricketer anywhere in the world who did not like Brian Statham as a person, as well as admiring him as a great bowler. He was a wonderful tourist both on and off the field. Brian was even-tempered and good company, threw a nifty dart, really enjoyed his food and drink and was more than a useful tennis player and never caused any trouble. In addition, he possessed a delightful sense of humour which was as dry as vintage Sancerre. He had the knack of coming out with a really succinct comment on life just when all the team were about to board some plane or bus at an uncivilised hour in the morning. At a private party on tour and late in the evening he specialised in making excellent pancakes which he tossed with all the panache of a television chef. Just like his catching in the deep, I never saw him put one down!

His two finest new ball partnerships in Test cricket were with Frank Tyson and Fred Trueman. His exceptional accuracy, often into the wind, ensured that runs were extremely hard to obtain and pressurised the unfortunate batsman, who at the other end was confronted by the extra speed of Frank, or more movement in the air or off the pitch from Fred.

If you asked any of the county captains during his long career to name the fast bowler they would most like to have in their side, at least ninety percent would have chosen Brian. In addition to his exceptional ability as a bowler, he was very economical, absolutely reliable, never temperamental and unlike a number of international quickies, was prepared to bowl his heart out in county matches, irrespective of the pitch or the conditions. In other words he was a great team man as well as a magnificent fast bowler. I was indeed fortunate to have spent so much time all over the world in his company.

Brian Close CBE

Brian made a dramatic entry into first-class cricket in 1949. This naturally gifted left-hand batsman, medium-pace and off-spin bowler did the 'double' for Yorkshire and made the first of his 22 Test appearances at the age of only 18. Later he developed into a brave and shrewd captain and under his astute leadership, Yorkshire won four Championship titles. He led England on seven occasions (won six, drew one) and played for Somerset between 1971 and 1977. Awarded the CBE for his services to the game, Brian returned to Yorkshire, after his playing days, to serve as Chairman of the cricket committee. An excellent soccer player he played for Leeds United, Arsenal and Bradford City, but after an injury, cricket claimed his talents in the summer of 1949.

Brian bowls to Brian in the 1968 Roses match

A TRIBUTE TO BRIAN STATHAM

My recollections of Brian Statham are many - I first met him on the 50-51 tour of Australia when he was flown out as a replacement half way through. He acquitted himself well on that occasion and from that moment on he was regarded as one of the best fast bowlers in the game, certainly the steadiest. When you batted against him you knew you would not get a moment's respite. He swung the ball in and on occasions rolled the ball away - he attacked your stumps. He was part of that wonderful fast bowling partnership with Freddie Trueman in the 50s and 60s that kept England at the top of the international cricket circuit in those years.

However, in 1963 the West Indies came to England with an array of talent in Sobers, Kanhai, Worrell, Butcher, Gibbs, Hall and Griffiths, to name but a few, the 1st Test was at Manchester, Brian's home ground. The wicket was so slow with no bounce and the W.I won the toss and batted and made 501 for 6 declared - no English bowler looked at all dangerous throughout the whole innings and the best analysis by any of our bowlers was 2 for 95 in 40 overs. After the second day the wicket disintegrated and took spin and England was bowled out twice for 205 and 296, Lance Gibbs taking 11 wickets for 157. I might point out that no fast bowler excelled or even looked dangerous during the whole match. Brian's bowling in that match was steady but because of the wicket his analysis of 0 for 121 in the 37 overs did not look good. As a result of this the selectors left him out of the team for the 2nd Test at Lord's (known then as the most receptive wicket in the country for fast bowlers) and replaced him with Derek Shackleton of Hampshire, a medium pace swing bowler. Throughout this Test match fast bowlers dominated the scene taking 32 of the 39 wickets to fall and the game finished in a memorable draw. However, I said on both occasions that had Brian Statham partnered Freddie at Lord's we would have won the game with ease. Freddie and Brian would have been too much of a handful for even the West Indies to cope with, no disrespect to Derek Shackleton but Brian's extra pace on that fiery wicket with the ridge, as it was then, enabling extra lift when bowling from the Pavilion end. I still maintain that the selectors choices after that 1st Test at Manchester cost us the series and it was Brian's "own" ground and wicket that brought about his demise from Test cricket. He was unfortunate.

I remember so many of our Roses matches at both Old Trafford and Headingley where Brian bowled wonderfully well, but no more so that in his last first-class match on August Bank holiday at Old Trafford 1968. He had elected to retire from the game after this Roses match. This time his "own ground" suited the fast bowler - Lancashire were bowled out for 162, our fast bowlers taking all 10 wickets. In Yorkshire's 1st

innings we were bowled our for a paltry 61 (my contribution being LBW b. Higgs 0).
Brian bowled brilliantly and had our batsmen in all kinds of trouble taking 6 for 34
in 18 overs. We then dismissed Lancashire's 2nd innings for 151 (our fast bowlers tak-
ing 7 of the wickets) and required 252 to win with our 2nd innings - Lancashire's bowl-
ing was "hot" - Brian Statham, supported by Ken Higgs and Ken Shuttleworth were a
real handful and hard to score off. We lost 3 wickets for 69, 4 for 148 and 5 for 159.
Just before the end of ordinary time (extra ½ hour to be claimed by either team if nec-
essary) we had achieved 189 for 5 and we hadn't enough time left to achieve our goal,
but Lancashire, if they could achieve another wicket could claim the extra ½ hour and
maybe go through our tailenders!

Brian was in full flight and he was to bowl the last over and I was at the receiving
end (on 77). Everyone trying their damnedest. I had to play every single ball of that
over that seemed to last for ages - Brian bowled a maiden. I needed all my skill to keep
him out and the result was a draw (honourable for both teams). As we went off the field
Brian for the very last time leading everyone towards the Pavilion. The Lancashire and
Yorkshire supporters giving him a standing ovation. I remarked to him, "I would have
liked to have been your last wicket in first-class cricket, but if I had done that you would
have claimed the extra half-hour and maybe won the match."

He appreciated the remark and smiled as he had always done throughout his career.

I will always remember Brian as a great adversary, a great colleague and a great
cricketer.

Lord Cowdrey of Tonbridge

Given the initial "MCC" by his father Colin
Cowdrey was coached by Ewart Astill at
Tonbridge School and was the youngest player at
13 years to play at Lord's. At 19 years he was also
the youngest player to collect a Kent cap. He represented Kent for 16 years and was a prolific
right-hand middle-order batsman of the highest
quality playing 402 matches and scoring 23,779
runs (average 42.01) with 58 centuries and a top
score of 250 v Essex at Blackheath in 1959. He
was Kent captain between 1957 and 1971. He
held 406 catches and made his Test debut in
1954-55 v Australia at Brisbane playing 114 Tests

and scoring 7,624 runs (average 44.06) with 22 centuries and he held 120 catches. He made 16 tours abroad and his highest score was 182 v Pakistan at The Oval in 1962. He captained England in 27 Tests with 8 victories. he scored a total of 42,719 runs with 107 centuries and was knighted for his services to cricket in 1992. He was President of MCC in 1987-88 and also the I.CC. He died in 2000 and his memorial service was held at Westminster Abbey.

Cricket is an extraordinary game which can bring out the best and the worst in those who play. Many regard it the best exercise there is for training character. It was Sir Frederick Toone who used these words of cricket. "It is a science, the study of a life time in which you may exhaust yourself, but never your subject. It is a contest calling for courage, skill, strategy and self-control. It is a contest of temper, a trial of honour, a revealer of character, including opportunities for courtesy, kindliness and generosity to an opponent".

The cynic revels in a statement of this sort, picking upon certain aspects and tearing them to shreds. He would, I venture to acclaim, find very tough opposition if he were to set his sights on Brian Statham! I have never ceased to admire the courageous way in which he accepted the role of supporting bowler to Frank Tyson in Australia. He was game to bowl into the wind, up the slope or at the end with bad footholds - and always uncomplaining. His skill was unquestionable.

I shall always recall his appreciation of strategy on many tours, when he would be pitted against fine batsmen, on their home wickets and there were not many runs to play with. Invariably, he would spot a batsman's strength and then bowl over after over with such accuracy as to forbid any scoring opportunities, and so often brought wickets to the bowler at the other end.

The Test. How many times have we seen or read sterling performances by Statham, only to find his final figures only telling half the truth. For him this was the test of temper and a trial of honour and he had displayed remarkable self control. The first ball

---

Tyson was the fastest, but Brian Statham of Lancashire and England was the most accurate. He rarely pitched short, preferring to concentrate on line and length, gaining movement off the wicket to make the batsman play at every delivery. You ignored a ball from Brian at your peril. Only occasionally would he slip in a bouncer, disguising it so cleverly that it brought him many wickets. Its trajectory would threaten the Adam's apple rather than the skull. It skimmed off the wicket.

Extract from Cricket and All That by Denis Compton, Pelham Books 1978.

---

of a fourth Test at Adelaide pitched on a perfect length outside the off stump, passed between McDonald's bat and pad only to miss the leg bail by a whisker. The greatest saint would have been forgiven an irate appeal to the heavens, but Brian was big enough to accept it quietly and smile!

This tribute was written by Colin Cowdrey in Brian's benefit year in 1961.

I am glad that you are going to produce a booklet. I just hope that all the contributors are able to do him justice - a great cricketer and a delightful personality. This is a speedy reply just to say that I shall be delighted to try and put something together and send this to you just as soon as I can.

Lord Cowdrey of Tonbridge

(Written on 24th November 2000)

Ted Dexter

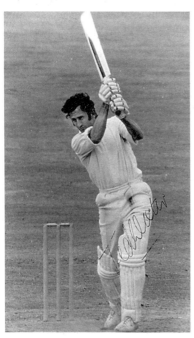

Ted Dexter, born in Milan, made his debut for Cambridge University in 1956 and played for Sussex from 1957 until 1968. He was a gifted all-round sportsman with a variety of interests. A dashing batsman of immense power, he relished driving the fastest bowling off either front or back foot. His fast-medium bowling was erratic but could be effective and he was a good fielder anywhere. He played in 62 Tests, 30 as captain, scoring over 4,000 runs and taking 66 wickets. He effectively retired from the game in 1965, aged 30, when he seemed to have many good years left, but played a couple of Tests in 1968. He stood unsuccessfully for Parliament against James Callaghan and returned to an active role in cricket as Chairman of Selectors from 1989 until 1993.

Brian Statham (or George, as we called him) was a Captain's dream. Either end, any time and a top quality effort was a certainty.

At Melbourne in 1963 he bowled through the hottest day like a Trojan. Returning to the dressing room, George removed his boots only. Taking a wooden chair and a can of beer to the showers, he sat under the cooling streams fully clothed enjoying his well earned drink and all the while audibly apologising to his feet!

Tom Graveney OBE

Tom Graveney was an elegant batting artist, a supremely graceful stylist whose cover-driving evoked memories of his Gloucestershire forebear Wally Hammond. Essentially a front-foot player, he used his height (6ft 1in) and reach to maximum effect and seldom went on to his back foot even to hook. It was only after leaving Bristol because of a captaincy dispute that he reached his peak at the highest level. Recalled to the Test arena in 1966 on his 39th birthday, he celebrated with a magnificent 96 against the fiery pace of Hall and Griffith. In 1964 and 1965 he had made vast contributions to Worcestershire's first Championships and he skippered them enthusiastically for three summers (1968 70) before taking up a coaching engagement in Brisbane. He enjoyed a long second career as a radio and television commentator with the BBC. He became President of Worcestershire in 1994 and was awarded the OBE. in 1968..

From the first time I met Brian on our MCC tour to India, Pakistan and Ceylon, we got on well, perhaps I'm flattering myself because he got on with everyone! We became firm friends and on my first major tours to West Indies and then Australia in 1954-55 we shared cabins and rooms.

As far as cricket was concerned he was one of the finest fast bowlers of all time. One of his greatest performances was not often remembered on that tour to Australia. Tyson with a 40 mph wind behind him destroyed the Australians at Sydney, but Brian bowled 20 odd 8 ball overs into that wind and took 3 for 39. I think he was tremendous. On another occasion in the Gents v Players at Lord's he was bowling at Bill Edrich, who never wore a thigh pad and never showed pain, and nipped the ball down the hill and hit him twice and with the last delivery hit him again. He smiled down the pitch at Bill and said "Go on Bill rub it, I know it hurts!"

On and off the field Brian with his dry sense of humour made friends and admirers all over the world and as Keith Miller would say "He was a good bloke." We will all miss him.

Sir Leonard Hutton

Born at Fulneck, one mile from Pudsey, Leonard Hutton was a right-hand batsman of peerless skill. Stylish with a wide range of strokes including a glorious cover-drive, he was a prince amongst batsmen. Hutton scored 40,140 first-class runs in his career including 129 centuries, 19 of which were Test hundreds. He was only 22 years of age when he made his 364 against Australia at The Oval in 1938. The first professional to captain England, Hutton was a shrewd skipper and under his leadership the Ashes were regained in 1953 and retained in Australia in 1954-55. Knighted for his services to cricket in 1956, Len won widespread affection as much for his personal charm as for the mastery of his batting. He died in 1990 and his memorial service was held in York Minster.

In the years immediately following the 2nd World War English cricket found itself considerably weakened though six years of inactivity. Many famous players had retired or had not returned from the war. Fast bowlers were virtually non-existent in a period when Lindwall and Miller put fear into the hearts of all batsmen.

Cyril Washbrook and myself gazed at the sky so often hoping a fast bowler would drop out of the blue to give that bite to England's attack without which no international side can hope to beat Australia. Injuries to bowlers on the 1950 tour in Australia caused the selectors to call for reinforcements and on the recommendation of Cyril Washbrook, Brian Statham flew from the depths of winter to the heat and humidity of Adelaide.

When this slim young Lancastrian with the build of a whippet rather than that of a fast bowler arrived, the supremacy of our ancient foe started to decline! The

A TRIBUTE TO BRIAN STATHAM

Australians were quick to see the potential quality of Brian but expressed a view that due to his slight build there must be some doubt as to his ability to stand the wear and tear of Test cricket on the cast iron pitches of Australia. Four years later, on those bone-hard grounds and concrete pitches of Melbourne and Adelaide, Brian bowled with the stamina of a lion, he was the senior partner in the Statham, Tyson partnership.

My first experience of Brian came during a Yorkshire v Lancashire match at Old Trafford. The pitch was perfect with little or no help for a fast bowler, but this youngster was as accurate as Lindwall. With experience his accuracy improved and he became the most accurate fast bowler whom I have played with or against. Brian later developed the out-swinger, and few bowlers have shaved the stumps so often, his luck at times has been deplorable; but never a moan or a harsh word nor a black look at the umpire or captain could be associated with Brian Statham. His wonderful record for England and Lancashire was remarkable - for much of his cricket had been played on the rain soaked pitches of Lancashire.

Let me take you to the scene of one of the finest spells of fast bowling I have seen. Georgetown is the place; the occasion of the historic bottle throwing incident. The ground is situated below sea level and can be hot, as it indeed was early in 1954. The West Indies had one of the strongest batting combinations international cricket had ever seen and batted on as good a wicket as any batsman could wish to find, in conditions most suitable to them.

The slip fielders hands perspired freely as Statham pounded over the hot turf to the wicket and 45 minutes of speed, hostility and super control of direction and Brian had broken the back of this magnificent West Indian batting!

Without this lead from the Lancashire lad our victory would not have been possible. It was the sort of lead Brian had always shown on the field, in the dressing room, hotel, train or plane. He proved himself as one of the most charming cricketers the game has seen.

No captain could have wished for more support than Brian gave to me at all times in England and overseas.

This tribute was written by Len Hutton in Brian's Benefit year in 1961

As a humble, fully paid-up member of the Fast Bowlers Union I pay homage to George, one of our most distinguished Life Vice-Presidents.

J J Warr

Alan Jones MBE

Alan Jones holds a strong claim to being Glamorgan's greatest batsman, with over 40,000 runs to his name in all forms of the game for his county. He scored 1,000 runs in 23 consecutive seasons and a county record of 52 centuries. With his prolific and consistant record, it is suprising that he was constantly overlooked by the England selectors. In 1970 he was chosen to play in the series against The Rest of the World. In 1982 he received the MBE in recognition of his devoted service to Welsh cricket.

Brian Statham, of Lancashire, was a totally different person to Fred, but certainly no less a bowler. He was phlegmatic, quiet and I don't think I ever heard him swear at a batsman. The first you saw of him was when he was bowling to you, unlike Fred, who seemed to have a season ticket to every home dressing room in the world before a match. He was a great bowler, very fast and accurate, seaming the ball off the wicket in both directions. He also thought about each delivery, playing on our weaknesses and he could tie the best batsmen down, forcing them to play at every ball and often inducing them to play and miss. It was incredible to think that two such different characters operated in tandem as possibly the most effective fast bowling spearhead England has ever had.

Peter Loader

Peter was born at Wallington in 1929. He was a right-arm fast bowler who represented Surrey between 1951 and 1963 where he formed part of the famous quartet (Bedser, Laker, Lock & Loader). He played in 13 Tests for England taking 39 wickets ave. 22.51. with a BB 6-36 v West Indies at Headingley in 1957 including the hat-trick. In 371 first-class matches he took 1,326 wickets ave. 19.04. He now lives in Australia.

I could recount many funny stories about "George", but let me say simply he was one of the nicest and kindest people I played with or against and I considered it a privilege that he chose me as a room-mate on our tours together.

I only wish some of our modern fast bowlers could behave as he did!

Peter May C.B.E.

Born in Reading in 1929, Peter May was coached at Charterhouse School by George Geary and played for Berkshire at 16 years. He made his first-class debut for Combined Services, before going up to Cambridge where he attained Blues in 1950, 1951 and 1952. He was considered the most talented right-handed strokemaking batsman to play in his era. Representing Surrey between 1950 and 1963 he played 388 first-class matches scoring 27,592 runs (average 51.00) with 85 hundreds. He played 66 Tests captaining in 41 with 21 wins and toured abroad on seven occasions. In his first Test at Headingley in 1951 he scored 138 v South Africa. In total he scored 4,537 runs (average 46.77). His highest score 285 n.o. was made in 1957 at Edgbaston against the West Indies. After retiring at 31 he concentrated on committee work and was an England selector between 1965 and 1968 and again between 1982 and 1988 as Chairman. He was awarded the CBE for services to cricket and he died in 1994.

I have had the great pleasure of sharing five overseas tours and playing in many Test matches with Brian Statham. He was certainly the most even tempered cricketer I have ever met. His composure hardly ever altered on the field of play and I regarded him as a model for any youngster. At times a bowler is greatly provoked by dropped catches and by batsmen playing and missing, but Brian took all this in his stride.

He was always ready to bowl another over or to have a rest if the situation demanded, and it assisted the captain greatly to have such co-operation. One of his finest days was at Lord's in June 1955 when we were playing the South Africans. I cannot exact-

ly remember how many overs he bowled from the pavilion end but I knew that our only hope of victory rested on his shoulders. Whenever I asked him to bowl just one more over I knew how exhausted he was, but there was never a word of complaint from him. A thunder cloud over the ground caused a dash for the pavilion and a little relief for him. I believe the score board showed his analysis to be 7-39. But that told only a very small part of the story.

Fast bowling is the most exacting role in cricket and Brian's motto had always been to conserve his energy and to attack the stumps. "If the batsman misses, then I shall hit", had been his creed as I had found to my cost when Surrey played Lancashire. He was very loose-limbed and his party piece consisted of clasping his hands behind his back and finishing with them still clasped in a similar position in front of him - most impressive! In fact this litheness was shown to excellent effect when we entered the fancy dress competition on one of our trips. We disguised ourselves as a calypso band and Brian entertained the company as a limbo dancer. It was most spectacular and we were rewarded with first prize.

Brian was a competent batsman and much underestimated. He had a remarkable eye and a very good temperament with some very good performances to his credit. Bob Appleyard and he made over 40 during the Sydney Test in 1954 and this partnership was a vital factor in our victory. On another occasion in Jamaica his overnight partner for the last wicket was David Allen and it was vital for us to bat as long as possible the following morning. Hall and Watson were at their fastest but both were faced with great courage by our two batsmen. Our innings lasted for another hour and we were able to save the match.

Brian had very definite views on the subject of net practice and I tried to persuade him to practice his batting. He hated batting in the nets and said that he didn't want to waste his runs there but to save them for the middle! He certainly did that, but I often wondered how many he might have made if he had bowled fewer overs.

I also regarded Brian as on of the finest out-fielders I have played with. There was a great thrill in picking up the ball on the boundary and returning it to the wicket-keeper right over the top of the stumps. In this respect fast bowlers were outstanding.

When catching, Brian had a quaint but most effective habit of circling under the ball before making the catch and I have seen him take some remarkable ones with this method.

This tribute was written by Peter May for Brian's benefit year in 1961.

Alan Oakman

Alan Oakman was one of England's tallest Test cricketers. He first played for Sussex in 1947 and in a career lasting until 1968 scored over 21,000 runs and took 736 wickets as well as holding 594 catches. He was better on hard wickets against pace bowling not of the quickest. He drove well and could defend for long periods, being very dependable in a crisis. He bowled off-spinners and was an outstanding catcher in the slips or at short leg. His Test career was limited to two appearances against Australia in 1956, when he caught five of Laker's nineteen victims at Old Trafford. He toured South Africa in 1956-7 where he was troubled with a back injury. After retiring he became a first-class umpire in 1969 and joined Warwickshire in 1970 as senior coach, a position he held until 1987.

Brian was very quiet and unassuming until he had a cricket ball in his hand - then he was lethal, though still quiet and focused on his bowling.

You could drive him for four or the ball would come back through your gate, pass over your middle/middle and off, and he would stand there hand on his hip with that deadpan expression, which was far more disconcerting than facing F.S. Trueman who, in his early days, was predictable. Hit him for four and you could tell by Fred's body and verbal language what was to follow - a bouncer, then Yorker. As he matured he became similar to Brian...well, not quite!

My final recollection of "George" was at Eastbourne in 1967. We were starting our second innings and he was taking his sweater off in that inimitable manner of his, one hand over his shoulder and behind his back, pulling his sweater up and over his head to hand to the umpire. I have never seen anybody perform this ritual in his unique way before or since. However..on with the story.

I mentioned to Brian that this was his last opportunity to get me out as I was to retire at the end of the season. Needless to say he did, as soon as I reached the other end. I would like to think it pitched middle, left me and I was caught behind, but to be honest I have a feeling I may have flashed at a wide one! As I walked away to the pavilion, I heard a voice say "And I have, Oakie".

I, too, was at his funeral and enjoyed seeing the many former Lancashire players I had played against during the '50s and '60s and, in particularl, Colin Cowdrey, his former England Captain, who had flown up from Arundel. The attendance of so many of his colleagues and friends is proof of the high esteem in which George was held.

Rt Rev Lord Sheppard of Liverpool

David Sheppard played for Sussex in 1947 while still at Sherborne School. Six feet tall, he was a stylish opening batsman with many graceful offside shots who possessed vast powers of concentration. He played for Cambridge University from 1950 to 1952 and was captain in the last year. He captained Sussex in 1953 and led them to second place in the Championship. He first played for England in 1950, being captain in two matches in 1954 and played the last of his 22 Tests in 1962-63. He was ordained in 1955 and played only occasionally afterwards, but scored a century for the Gentlemen in 1962 and went on MCC's tour of Australia in 1962-63. He was Suffragan Bishop of Woolwich from 1969 to 1975, and then became Bishop of Liverpool. Had he not gone into the Church so early, he would have undoubtedly added to his tally of 15,838 runs and 45 centuries. He has now retired and is a Vice-President of Lancashire CCC and was made President of Sussex CCC in 2001.

Brian Statham and Roy Tattersall were flown out to replace injured bowlers in the middle of the 1950-51 Tour of Australia. Straight from midwinter in England, their first outing was in a country match at Renmark. The temperature was 103 and a hot wind was blowing. Brian just about made it to the wicket himself, and the ball just reached the bat!

Nevertheless, he didn't bowl a bad ball. I looked up the scores and I see that he bowled 10 overs for 16 runs and one wicket.

Brian was always the most supportive team man. In Australia in 1962-3, I had a bad time in the field. I had dropped two sharp chances in the Melbourne Test. Now at Sydney I dropped a real "gaper" from Neil Harvey. In the middle of the pandemonium with the crowd whooping at the miss, I wanted the ground to open up and hide me. Brian was next to me in the field and mouthed "bad luck", making me feel the support a good team can offer.

M. J. K. Smith OBE

Michael John Knight Smith OBE first made the news when scoring centuries for Oxford in each of his three University matches. After a few games for Leicestershire Smith joined Warwickshire and from 1957 until 1967 was a popular county captain. A heavy scorer from the outset, he won the first of his 50 Test caps against New Zealand in 1958. Though a Test record of 2278 runs, average 31.63, confirmed that he was not invariably happy against top-class pace, he played many fine innings, including 3 centuries while on 25 occasions he was a captain who won the genuine respect of friend and foe alike. For Warwickshire, he gave many years of outstanding service and finally retired in 1975 with a record of 39832 runs, average 41.84, with 69 centuries. His 593 catches reflected possession of one of the safest pair of hands in cricket - despite the need to wear spectacles for the whole of his first-class career. He became a Committee member and later Chairman at Warwickshire. He was manager of the England team in the West Indies in 1993/4.

The ability to bowl fast is offered to very few people - by fast I mean by international standards. I also mean to contrive to bowl over the season and seasons, home and abroad. First the ability and then the commitment to do it. Few have the heart for it long term and even less are named without any reservations.

Quite simply Brian was a gem; no limitations, no reservations. He had a great abil-

ity and consistently gave it all. What will appear in all these tributes to his bowling will be talk of his accuracy. His philosophy was so simple "If he misses I hit". I doubt anyone has ever been more accurate at his pace. As a batsman you knew you had to get bat on ball. There just wasn't going to be any rest period watching the wide deliveries fly by and be wasted.

A great player must, almost by definition, be a "one off". Brian really did appear to be too good to be true. A players' player, a gift to a captain and a major player on all the world's great arenas.

If Lancashire could replicate one player - no contest - who would come second? And England would be in very close attendance.

Raman Subba Row CBE

Having enjoyed a highly successful sports career at Whitgift School, Raman Subba Row had little difficulty in gaining blues for cricket (all three years) and rugby fives at Cambridge. A tall and extremely sound left-handed opening or middle-order batsman. He was an excellent fielder, usually at slip but equally effective at gully or in the deep. He celebrated being captain of Northamptonshire (1958-61) by scoring 300 against his former county. He met with considerable success in Test cricket, scoring a valuable hundred in his first match overseas and adding other centuries in his first and last matches against Australia. He retired rather prematurely from first-class cricket to devote himself to his public relations business but has seldom been far from cricket administration in the last two decades. In addition to managing the 1981-82 tour of India, he has served on the MCC committee and been chairman of Surrey., As chairman of the TCCB he was splendidly progressive and has showed qualities of tireless, determined and skilful diplomacy.

I was lucky enough to play with and against "George" for England and in the County Championship and we had many happy times together.

My first Test match was at Old Trafford v New Zealand in 1958. It rained very hard on day 4 (Monday) whereupon George assumed that there would be no further play that day or on day 5 (Tuesday). As a result we all went out to a party in Cheshire and when the sun shone on Tuesday morning, the match started on time and we all had to take our monster hangovers on to the field with us. Thank heavens we won but that was the last of George's weather forecasting!

In a County match (Lancashire v Northamptonshire), by which time after two over-seas tours I had got to know George very well, the light deteriorated whilst we (Northants) were batting, but we wanted to stay on because we were in a good position to win the match. As it got darker and darker George bowled me a bouncer which removed my cap (no helmets in those days!) and we ran 1 leg bye. As I reached the other end George put his hands to his head and said to me "Raman, please don't do that again". He thought that he was going to hit me straight between the eyes with that deliv-ery and was genuinely concerned for my safety. That was a true reflection of his real char-acter.

Freddie Trueman OBE

Fred Trueman made his county debut in 1949. This tearaway quick bowler devel-oped into one of the most feared fast men in the world game during the 1950s and 60s. A copy-book action and ideal physique for fast bowling, he could bowl late out-swingers and off-cutters at pace if the pitch suited. A somewhat flam-boyant but entertaining batsman he had a good defence and in the field he was an excellent backward short-leg. The first bowler to take 300 Test wickets, his 2304 first-class victims came at the economical average of 18.29 apiece. In retirement, Fred became a well known TV personality and much respected BBC radio com-mentator and journalist. Awarded the OBE in 1989, the honour was richly deserved.

It was a sad day in June 2000 when I received the news of the sad passing of my for-mer bowling partner Brian Statham (known as George).

We had many great times and laughs together, moments I will never forget.

One such day occurred in British Guiana, West Indies in 1960. We had spent all that day talking about cricket when George pulled back the curtains and said "it's dark". He then said "There is a western film on at the cinema tonight, shall we go?" I agreed and when we later met up with Geoff Pullar and Tommy Greenough in the lobby of the hotel they decided to join us.

We arrived at the cinema and went to sit in the balcony seats and settled down to watch the film. We all fell about with laughter when some of the West Indian audience was standing up and shouting to the "Good guy" on the screen "look out, the baddie is behind you".

During the showing of the film a pleasant young lady came along with a tray of ice creams etc. As she approached us she shone her torch on to the tray and asked if we would like to purchase any of the items on display. George replied "Thank you but it would be better if you brought four lagers". The lady left us with a giggle and went about her business.

We all had a laugh too but were somewhat surprised when about fifteen minutes later she reappeared with four beers!

Brian paid for them and after thanking her suggested she should repeat the procedure in another fifteen minutes, which she did.

Just one of the very happy memories of my "Old mate, George".

Frank Tyson

On his day Frank Tyson was one of the fastest bowlers in world cricket. Born in Lancashire in 1930, he played 170 matches for Northamptonshire and 17 Test matches, including all five in the 1954/55 series in Australia which saw England retain the Ashes. He now lives and coaches in Australia

Modest, loyal, honest friend

Fiery Fred Trueman was the cult figurehead of England's fast bowling renaissance of the 1950s. But the other Test quickies of this era, men line Alan Moss, "Scrubs" Loader and myself, knew that the real engine room of inspiration was to be found at The Oval and Old Trafford manned by Alec Bedser and Brian Statham. So "George", as we bid farewell to you in 2000, I want to acknowledge your efforts on behalf of the boys in the national team of that wonderful decade, especially your 18-wicket contribution to England's 3-1 triumph in the 1954/55 Ashes series Down Under.

On a personal plane I thank you for your unflagging bowling support from the other end. My 28 wickets in that rubber were in no small part due to the eagerness of the Australian batsmen to escape from your speedy attentions. And what about your batting in Sydney's Second Test? Our slender 38-run victory there was made possible when you and Bob Appleyard added 46 in 50 minutes for the last wicket of our second knock.

When it came to bowling Australia to defeat in the final innings, you were there again, bursting your lungs to bowl for 85 minutes into the wind, as I surfed downwind. Together we destroyed the Australian batting for 184.

It was the same story in Melbourne, you breasting the breeze for nearly an hour and a half to take 2 for 19 in the final Australian knock of 111; thus allowing me to coast downwind and pick up 6 for 16 at the other end. And when we won the match by 128 runs, your modesty was such that as we left the field you hung back in the body of the team, reluctant to accept your due recognition, I had to wait for you to draw abreast before I could place my arm around your shoulder and we could leave the field as we bowled: together.

In the deciding Fourth Test in Adelaide, we surprised all the pundits who, when Appleyard dismissed Morris, Harvey and Burke for 13 on the fourth day, expected the spinners to do all the terminal damage in Australia's final knock. They never even got a bowl. Instead, it was you with 3 for 12 and myself with 3 for 17 who pressed home

our psychological advantage and mopped up the opposition in a breathtaking hour and a half.

Your accuracy was such that on that 1954/55 Australian tour you took 6 for 0 against a South Australian Country XI in Mount Gambier, all of them direct hits on the stumps worthy of a Smart Missile. Small wonder, then, that Neville Cardus, the journalist, queried when you retired in 1969 whether you had ever bowled a wide. (In fact in the greener days of your 19 years at Lancashire you sent down 40)

And although you were supposed to be much slower than I, when our speeds were measured at the aeronautical college in Wellington, New Zealand, in wet and slippery conditions, you locked in at an inaccurate 87 mph, only 2 mph behind my 89 mph. But you had much more than speed. Just a couple of variations were your nip-backer - that venomous back-break off what you used to call a "nasty, nagging length" - and your "chop 'em off at the ankle yorker".

So it's valé, dear George. I shall always remember your pep-talk to your poor bloodied feet propped up on the dressing-room table at the tea interval: "Come on lads, just another two hours to go and I can put you up for the night." And I shall never forget your breakfast of "a fag, a cough and a cup of coffee". Or your preference for a celebration ale instead of the "soda pop" of champagne. You were a modest, loyal, honest and humorous friend, when all those qualities were essential to the make-up of "a great cricketer".

In a way, I am glad that you did not live to see cricket the way you played it completely discredited and degraded by more accusations of fraudulent betting and match-fixing. "Kipper" Cowdrey spoke for us all when he said: "If my son ever became a professional cricketer, I hope he would be like Brian Statham."

Richie Benaud OBE

Richie Benaud ranks among the great Test captains, as well as being one of the finest all-rounders ever produced by Australia. To his considerable talents as a leg-spin and googly bowler, forcing right-hand bat and specialist close fielder, were later added tactical skills and qualities of leadership of the highest order. He became the first player to take 200 Test wickets and score 2000 Test runs in the history of the game. He finished with 248 wickets. He led Australia in six series, winning five and drawing one. Now a well respected journalist and television commentator for Channel 4 in England and Channel 9 in Australia.

Brian was one of the finest players ever to turn out for England and one of the best people on and off the field.

My two great memories of him, apart from sitting in the dressing-room and having the occasional beer and chatting, were in 1958-59 and 1961. In 1958-59 Fred Trueman was unable to play in the First and Second Test matches because of what nowadays would be classed as stress fractures in the back, but forty years ago related merely to lumbago!

Brian turned in one of the greatest performances I have ever seen at the MCG in the Second Test where he restricted Australia to a 49-run first innings lead with bowling figures of 26-6-57-7. When I walked into the England dressing-room with a beer in my hand, he was sitting quietly with a beer in his, looking at his feet and saying "Sorry feet." Then, in 1961, in the Old Trafford Test, he turned in one of the great bowling spells of all time in Ashes' battles, taking 5/53 from 21 overs where hardly anyone but Bill Lawry and Brian Booth managed to play him with the middle of the bat.

He was Frank Tyson's partner in the devastating fast bowling combination in 1954-55 and he was what Australians like to call a 'good bloke'.

Sir Donald Bradman

The greatest cricketer of the 20th century. Born in new South Wales in 1908. One of the greatest batsmen in the history of the game, he played for Australia from 1928 to 1948 (captain 1936-48). A prodigious scorer, he made the highest aggregate and largest number of centuries in Tests against England and holds the record for the highest Australian Test score against England (334 at Leeds in 1930). His batting average in Test matches was an astonishing 99.94 runs per innings. The first Australian cricketer to be knighted (in 1949). He was chairman of the Australian Cricket Board 1960-63 and 1969-70. He died in 2001 and all Australia mourned its favourite son.

It was an honour to pay tribute to Lancashire's lion hearted fast bowler, Brian Statham. I saw Brian bowl on the first occasion that he had participated in a first-class match in Australia and the circumstances were worth recording.

Freddie Brown's 1950-51 team was in trouble and it was decided to seek reinforcements. The choice had fallen on two Lancashire bowlers, Tattersall and Statham, who were flown out to assist their colleagues. Just imagine the situation! A dyed-in-the-wool Lancastrian was "enjoying" the Manchester atmosphere in the middle of winter - biting, penetrating damp cold - fogs - smog - thick woollen clothes - warm fires - even watching favourite soccer teams. Suddenly the scene was changed by a flight of some 12,000 miles in two days to Adelaide where the temperature was 105 degrees in the shade, the air dry and sometimes dust laden.

The air journey itself was strenuous and, from personal experience, I think one required a few days to recover from it. Changes in meal hours, times of sleeping and waking - the human body had to re-adjust itself. Those things alone on top of the sudden switch from winter to summer would have more than taxed the physical fitness of Herb Elliott. No wonder Brian had complained that he experienced some difficulty in breathing when he first bowled on the Adelaide Oval.

For good measure it had been Brian's first experience in bowling eight balls to the over. It could scarcely have been expected that he would cause a sensation but his 16 overs in that game produced two wickets and only 37 runs. Since then I have watched Brian bowl probably thousands of balls and his career has been notable for confirming the impression of accuracy and economy which formed that opening day in Australia.

At first glance one perceived that Brian's delivery was somewhat unusual. He did not use the body swing to the same extent as Freddie Trueman. Yet his delivery gave the impression of a deliberate aiming at a target, which he seemed to hit most effectively.

Since that day in Adelaide in 1951, Australia's batsmen developed a growing respect for Brian's bowling which, like wine, appeared to improve with age!

This tribute was written by Don Bradman in Brian's Benefit Year in 1961

Jackie McGlew

Jackie McGlew became synonymous with South African cricket in the 1950's his batting befitting his name: he was a sticker, and he became famous - or notorious for some of Test cricket's slowest innings. He batted nine hours 35 mins. for 105 against Australia at Durban in 1957/58. He played in 34 Tests for South Africa scoring 2,440 runs ave 42.06. with 7 centuries.

He played for Natal between 1947-1967 (86 matches) scoring over 5,000 runs ave. 46.49. He managed the Under 19 tour to West Indies in 1991-92. He loved writing and died in 1998.

Brian Statham was cricket's Richard the Lionheart! In many ways I was sorry that he preferred to be called George and couldn't imagine why, unless it was because he was England's patron saint of bowling. Make no mistake, Brian had a heart as big as Old Trafford itself and there were times without number when he carried England and Lancashire to success on the strength of his own supple shoulders.

We South Africans had special reasons for regarding the Lancashire and England fast bowler as our special enemy. Time and time again he had swung into action and sent our wickets hurtling out of the ground. His greatest triumph against us was undoubtedly at Lord's on that historic occasion when he took 7 - 39 and almost bowled himself into the ground!

He must have been one of the finest and fastest bowlers England has ever produced. Like all really great bowlers he was always attacking you. As a batsman opening the innings I've had my share of Brian and knew of nobody more accurate, more hostile or more dangerous.

He moved with the agility, strength and speed of a black panther - and yet, off duty, he was a grand chap to know and to respect. Once play had ended for the day Brian turned from fiery fast bowler to a really good companion of cricket.

In the field Brian was rightly rated as one of the safest catchers in the business. He was also one of cricket's deadliest throwers and there were many batsmen who lived to regret a tendency to take one for the throw when the ball had been within reach of Brian. He was left-handed and unambitious. If he ever got ideas about scoring a thousand runs in a season he'd probably have done it. I saw him hold up many an England innings and produce some near-classical shots into the bargain.

This tribute was written by Jackie McGlew in Brian's Benefit year in 1961.

Bobby Simpson

Bobby Simpson made his debut for NSW at the age of 16. In 1963 he made his career best 359. He retired from first-class cricket at the age of 31, but found himself being called back some ten years later -in the Packer period to captain both his country and NSW. In all he played 257 first-class matches making over 21,000 runs at an average of 56 with 60 centuries and 12 double centuries including 311 at Old Trafford in 1964. He played 62 times for Australia, 39 as captain scoring over 5,000 runs and was regarded as one of the finest slip fielders in the game with 110 Test catches. He managed Australia to a World Cup victory in 1987 and is currently coach at Lancashire. His father played football for Stenhousemuir in Scotland.

He was a great fast bowler. Not only did I play against him, but I had the good fortune to be in the same side on occasions. I toured with him in the Commonwealth team and at that stage of my career was struggling for form. I had been dropped by Australia, came to play in the Lancashire League and tried to change from a middle order dasher to opening batsman. Brian gave me plenty of advice and encouragement on how to change my technique in order to face fast bowlers with confidence.

He was a magnificent contributor to cricket at all levels. He always had time to talk to youngsters and sign autographs. Down under we thought of him as a "Good bloke." He always associated with the opposition and after close of play was first into the dressing room to have a chat and a drink.

One summer when I was with the India World Cup team I met up with Brian and enjoyed an hour reminiscing about our playing days. His performances with Lancashire and England were incredible. His reputation as the most accurate fast bowler cannot be disputed and some of our young quickies find it hard to believe that he took over eighteen hundred wickets for the county. It is far beyond their comprehension. Those wickets were a testament not only to his ability, but to the pressure he exerted on batsmen.

I do not think he had an enemy within the game. He was a superb bowler, a lot faster than he looked, and always a gentleman - even when he aimed a bouncer at you. I will remember him as a very nice person on and off the field.

PART FOUR

Statham in the Media

Brian with Neville Cardus

E.W.Swanton OBE, CBE

Jim Swanton was one of the most authoratative cricket writers in the 20th Century and wrote about cricket for over 60 years. He worked on the London Evening Standard from 1927-39 and during the war was imprisoned by the Japanese in Thailand. From 1946 he was cricket correspondent of the Daily Telegraph and also broadcast for the BBC Test Match commentaries for 40 years. He wrote many cricket books and for his services to cricket he was appointed OBE in 1965 and CBE in 1994 and a Life Vice President of MCC in 1989. He died in 2000.

England's Best Since Harold Larwood

My first recollection of Brian is of meeting him on the players' balcony at The Oval while Lancashire were playing Surrey in the match that decided the championship (inconclusively, as it turned out) in 1950. One noticed his quiet, laconic talk, with the half-smile never far away, the supple, but dangerously spare frame of this apparently up-and-coming fast bowler. On physical grounds that day it was difficult not to prefer, as an investment for the future, the chances of T E Dickinson with whom he shared the new ball.

The next time we met, as fate would have it, was a few months later at the break-fast table of the Royal Sydney Golf Club where Brian and Roy Tattersall pitched up for a day or two's acclimatisation before resuming the journey from Manchester to Adelaide. It will be remembered that M.C.C. who, apart from Len Hutton and sometimes F. R. Brown could not get any runs but shared an astonishing facility in the Test matches for getting Australia out cheaply, had sent at the pinch for two more bowlers. Though Brian did not play in either of the remaining two Tests, Tattersall did.

Furthermore, wearing MY boots - for his feet had swollen in the tropical heat - he had a great deal to do with England's first post-war victory over Australia by staying there with Reg Simpson with whom he put on 74 for the last wicket.

Young Brian observed these proceedings from the narrow slit which is the players' outlook on the world from the Melbourne dressing-room. Little can so modest a fellow have dreamed that four years later he and Frank Tyson would be cheered off that very ground for a display of fast bowling which, to the astonishment of friend and foe, had put England ahead in the rubber and paved the way for our only Ashes victory in Australia in quarter of a century!

The surpassing merit of Brian as a bowler was that he consistently maintained, day in, day out - season in, season out - such an astonishingly high standard. There has never been a straighter fast bowler; there has not been a more accurate one in English cricket since Harold Larwood. Utter dependability coupled with an easy, unruffled temperament were his hallmarks.

But one remembers certain standing things. There was his extraordinary performance at Lord's in '55 when South Africa went in in the fourth innings to make 183 to win. Brian bowled from the Pavilion end unchanged for 29 overs for the first seven wickets before Wardle polished off the tail and 29.12.39.7 were the figures that brought England victory out of the blue after being 171 behind on first innings.

As an example of combined skill and stamina I doubt if Brian has bettered the performance which, with Tyson's, won the Sydney Test of 1954. Tyson had the better record: ten wickets in the game to Brian's five - but the latter wheeled up over after over, running and bowling full into the teeth of the half-gale that Tyson had at his back.

Brian indeed has been a credit to his fellow-cricketers and the game of cricket. He proved himself one of the fast bowlers of history.

David Frith

David Frith, cricket writer and magazine editor, writing and compiling almost a library of books single-handedly. David also founded the popular Wisden Cricket Monthly and was Editor from 1979 to 1996. His autobiography "Caught England Bowled Australia" helps explain his intimate knowledge of cricket and cricketers in both countries.

The Model Professional

Some English cricketers have been popular in Australia, believe it or not, and none more so than Brian Statham. He made three full tours of Australia, and I watched in admiration as he gave his all in five Test matches in Sydney in that time, usually bowling into the breeze while Frank Tyson, Trevor Bailey or Fred Trueman benefited at the opposite end. I can't recall one single word of disapproval from any of the vocal spectators around me on the Hill or in the Sheridan Stand in all that time. He was simply the model professional cricketer, doing his duty with a faint smile and the occasional shrug, returning to his fielding position at third man, in front of that notorious Hill, where he always raised a cheer of appreciation.

Brian was just so easy-going, relaxed and deceptively casual. As a 17-year-old I was so keen that one evening in 1955 I found my way out to the English team's hotel in Coogee and sat watching them in the communal lounge. Brian had his tired old feet up on the metal table. From a watching brief that must have lasted at least an hour, that is the image I remember most of all - together with Denis Compton's loud call to a passing waiter "Four beers, please, waiter!"

I was also fascinated by a member of England's Bodyline side 20-odd years earlier, the baggageman/scorer, George Duckworth.

Perhaps strangest of all, beyond the vivid recollection of that unique acceleration to the bowling crease and rubbery delivery of a rapid ball, limbs defying gravity, is Brian's batting, which abides in memory. The most wonderful Test match of all the hundreds in my memory-bank remains the second Test of the 1954-55 Ashes series at the SCG, won by England by 38 runs. Note the margin of victory.

Peter May scored a century and Frank Tyson took 10 wickets in the match despite being knocked cold by a Lindwall bouncer. But in England's first innings in this low-scoring match Brian and Wardle put on 43 for the 10th wicket; and in the second Brian and Appleyard put on 46. Brian took five wickets in this thriller and bowled bravely. But it was his left-handed batting resistance that annoyed the Australians even more.

Four years later, as we watched the Melbourne Test through the new wonder of television, we saw Brian take 7 for 57 - only for England's position to be scuppered in a couple of hours by Ian Meckiff, who took 6 for 38, consigning England - with Alan Davidson's help - to an all-out total of 87 and inexorable defeat. Poor old "George" soon had to put his boots back on and trudge out to bat at No 10, just when he must have been hoping for a full day's rest at least.

He gave his all at all times of course, though I did once spot him taking it easy during an England net practice in Sydney. He was bowling off three or four paces and yet he was still jarring the bat occasionally - and once dropped one short and sent the ball soaring clean over the rear netting. My mates and I struggled to manage that off 17 paces.

I saw little of Brian after he retired. Then Fred organised that gala function in London in 1989. Walking from my car to the Grosvenor House, I spotted someone in a dinner jacket whom I had last seen in flannels and that proud MCC touring sweater years ago. He was just standing there in a kind of dream, so I blurted out "Brian, how are you, shouldn't you be inside?"

The fact of the matter was that he was taking in the spring-time air that evening in Park Lane - notwithstanding the car exhaust fumes - just minding his own business as usual. But some daft non-cricketing police officer had questioned him. Seems he looked like he was loitering. "And know what?" said Brian. "He seemed worried that I was a terrorist!"

A less likely terrorist there never had been. He always bowled his heart out; never bounced tailenders - simply sent them packing with his God-given skill as a purveyor of swinging yorkers; and deserved more than most the stupendous testimonial that awaited him under the glittering chandeliers that night in London.

Colin Shindler

Colin Shindler is the author of 'Manchester United Ruined My Life', a homage to Manchester City and Lancashire. He went to Bury Grammar School and Gonville & Caius Cambridge where he remained after graduation to complete a PhD thesis on Hollywood and the Great Depression. He wrote the movie screenplay for the film 'Buster' and has written and produced television series such as 'Lovejoy', 'A Little Princess' and 'Wish me Luck'. His latest book is 'Fathers, Sons and Football'.

The modest idol who entranced Lancashire

With the death of the greatest of all my youthful heroes, Brian Statham, a part of my childhood feels like it has vanished. To me, and I dare say to every other middle-aged Lancastrian who cherishes the cricket of his native county in his soul, his premature death at the age of 69 will have come as a terrible shock.

They are all gone now, that team of our early youth: Washbrook and Grieves, Ikin and Hilton, Dyson and Wharton. Now the greatest of them all has joined them.

Brian Statham was our idol for all the right reasons that great sportsmen should become heroes. He combined outstanding achievement with an uncomplaining willingness to bowl all day uphill into the wind so that Tyson and Trueman could steal the headlines. Whether it was on the flat pitches of the West Indies and Australia or on a green top at Chesterfield, Brian Statham bowled his heart out for his country and his county and we loved him for it.

No matter how many times he went past the outside edge or saw the ball bisect the slips, he never posed with outrage as many of his contemporaries and all of his successors now do, hands on hips, a volley of abuse aimed indiscriminately at batsmen, fielders, umpires and God. He walked back to his mark knowing perfectly well that the next ball was more than likely to knock the middle stump out of the ground.

On a bitterly cold April day in the Parks, Statham bowled the first ball of the match against Oxford University. It drew Duncan Worsley, the future Lancashire opener, into a groping prod. The ball whipped away, missing bat and off stump by a fraction of an inch and thumped into the wicketkeeper's gloves.

An embarrassed Worsley kept his head down, waiting for the traditional cutting remark of the opening bowler. He looked up to find Statham four yards away smiling gently. "Good morning!" he said kindly.

I spent whole days of my summer holidays imitating his distinctive windmill action. We lived in a semi-detached house with a longish drive and a garage at the end on whose doors were permanently chalked three stumps.

To achieve the full majesty of that run-up, shirt filling with breeze, I really needed to start in the driveway of No 15 but the Grosskopfs who lived there were not cricket lovers and didn't appreciate the importance of the fast-bowlers rhythm so the nine-year-old Brian Statham was reduced to bowling permanently off his short run.

It pained us that Statham's action was deemed insufficiently classical as compared with that of Fred Trueman. To us it was an aesthetic delight, an awesome thing of beauty. Trueman's looked like the pumping piston of a steam engine in comparison.

We were conscious too of how often in Test matches Statham was brought back to bowl to a batsman when he was on 98 or 99 whereas Trueman was never subjected to this indignity.

I always believed that captaining Lancashire was the easiest job in the world, comprising as it did the one task of throwing the ball to Brian Statham. From 11.30 in the morning until 12.40 Statham bowled eight or so overs from the Stretford end, at which point the opposition would be struggling on 33 for two, Statham having taken both wickets. Somehow we bumbled along for half an hour until Statham came back at ten past one for three overs before lunch.

When play resumed at ten past two he was ready to bowl all afternoon, pausing perhaps only to bowl from the City end for a change of scenery. Frankly, had it been legally permissible for him to have bowled from both ends throughout the day we would have been delighted and it is doubtful if he would have demurred.

In these pages many years ago Neville Cardus reported of Wilfred Rhodes that he considered himself "nivver a star - just a good utility player." That would probably have been Statham's self-assessment as well.

He would have been wrong. He was a bright shining star to all of us who gazed at him in adoration, the greatest Lancastrian bowler who ever drew breath.

Derek Hodgson

Derek Hodgson reported Lancashire Cricket from 1958 for the Daily Express and The Independent. He has written a History of Yorkshire Cricket and is also Editor of the Yorkshire CCC Yearbook. He is secretary of The Cricket Writers Club.

If ever there was a natural champion it was Brian Statham. He arrived in cricket at Old Trafford in June 1950, literally out of the blue of the Royal Air Force, an unknown fast bowler who had been recommended by the RAF and by his local league club, Denton West. Such was his astonishing impact on the county game that seven months later he was being flown out to reinforce the England team, then, as now, struggling in Australia.

Lancashire had begun that summer thinking they had a crisis to meet with the retirement, real and impending, of their two senior seamers, Eddie Phillipson and Dick Pollard. The long lean 20 year-old Statham was pressed into first team service and at Bath in July had the telegraphic machines chattering by dismissing five Somerset batsmen, four bowled, for five runs in seven overs.

It was as if he had sprung, fully armed, from the earth in the manner of a Greek myth. He had it all: speed, stamina, a quickly developing ability to make the ball seam off the pitch both ways and, above all, the virtue that made him world-class in a matter of months and kept him in the front rank of world bowlers for almost two decades, devastating accuracy. "If they miss, I hit," he was to put it simply later on, and few truer words have been spoken in cricket.

Statham was a born athlete, loose-limbed and double-jointed, a footballer good enough to have had trials as a winger with Manchester United. He grew up in Gorton with Roger Byrne, left back and captain of the Busby Babes.

Statham's relentless line of attack, over after over, contributed enormously to the success of his two most famous partners, Fred Trueman and Frank Tyson. Batsmen never

122

knew what to expect from "Fiery" and the "Typhoon"; after six deliveries from Statham, when they knew that a fraction of an error in judgement would bring the death rattle, they were too often tempted into adventure against more extravagant deliveries, with equally fatal results, caught behind or at slip.

"The Rapier and the Broadsword" was one broadsheet description of the Statham-Trueman partnership. "Raffles and Bill Sykes" was an Old Trafford pavilion comment, made outside the hearing of any Yorkshireman.

Statham was more than just fast and straight. On a desultory first afternoon of a three-day match against Nottinghamshire at Trent Bridge there was a sudden commotion from the home dressing room, loud enough to cause the press to investigate. "It's Stat," reported our enquirer. "He bowled a half-volley and our lads had never seen that before."

By 1953 he was always among the first choices for England. He finished above Trueman in the tour averages for West Indies in 1953-54 and was given a new partner, Tyson, another Lancastrian who had been allowed to slip away to Northamptonshire, for Hutton's tour of Australia in 1954-55.

England, playing four fast bowlers, an unheard-of strategy in the 1950s, crashed disastrously in the first Test at Brisbane but after that Tyson's awesome speed, Statham's penetration, supported by excellent spin bowling, brought England a series of glittering victories and the Ashes. Tyson won the fame and adulation while Statham, as usual, was happy to stand to one side.

His figures spoke loudly enough. Against Glamorgan at Cardiff, 6-12. "He's too bloody fast," a disconsolate batsman told Eric Todd of the Guardian that day. Against Leicestershire at Hinckley: 6-20. Against Leicestershire at Grace Road: 14-58. Against Warwickshire at Coventry 8-34 and 7-55. Most of these feats were performed on better pitches than are seen today. Especially pleasing was a Roses match at Old Trafford in 1960 when he appealed six times for lbw against Yorkshire and won every time.

He wasn't much for nets and practising, the fast bowlers of his day reckoning that 28 first-class three-day games was enough. His stature was such that legends grew in his shadow. Like Trueman he never seemed to lose fitness or form and on one occasion, when he was recovering from a strain, selectors pondered on whether he should play.

Summoned from the dressing room, not having changed, he was invited to demonstrate by bowling at a single stump. He took off his jacket, loosened his tie, laid his cigarette on the grass, took two steps and knocked the stump out of the ground. The selectors smiled and joked: "Ah, but can you do it again?" Statham shrugged, did it again, put on his jacket, picked up his cigarette and strolled off. He played.

Lancashire were always having captaincy crises in the 1960s and it was only after advertising for, and failing to find, an amateur that they turned in 1965 to their most distinguished player who, I suspect, saw the job as a duty rather than a preference, having collected £13,000 in a testimonial three years earlier.

His vice-captain was David Green, an Oxford Blue, and the pair brought a spirit of adventure and humour to county cricket that has been rarely matched. The Lancashire team of that time contained enough talent to have won the championship several times and purists might complain that as professionals they were too easy-going. Perhaps so, but fewer jollier bands have ever laughed and sung their way through the shires and, win, lose or draw, they were always entertaining. Lancashire were the silk, steel and lace Cavaliers to Brian Close's Roundheads across the Pennines.

Statham was known as "George" to his friends and "the Whippet" or "Greyhound" to his opponents, a decent description of his style. He was modest, polite and courteous even when faced with the most asinine of press questions and no matter what the result, always made himself available afterwards, a discipline emulated by few county captains of that time.

He retired in 1968 and said, confidentially, afterwards that he would have liked to continue a little longer but could not face the prospect of more one-day cricket. He had played in 70 Test matches, taking 252 wickets for England, one memorable performance coming at Lord's in 1955. South Africa needed 183 to win but were dismissed for 111, Statham bowling unchanged for 29 overs to take 7-39.

He was a stubborn left-handed tail-end batsman and outfielder with a magnificent arm and a safe catch. In all he took 2,260 wickets at an average of 16.36. "I was lucky to be playing cricket for a living. And there were such a lot of nice people around."

He later became a brewery representative, served Lancashire as a member of the committee and as President and is commemorated at Old Trafford in the Washbrook-Statham Stand and in an office block on the periphery. He was appointed CBE in 1966 when his services for England deserved an earldom.

Reprinted from the Independent by permission of the Editor, Simon Kelner.

Brian Statham

by Michael Parkinson

(written for *The Sunday Times* in 1967)

I first saw him in those distant days when people used to queue to see a cricket match. We were standing outside Old Trafford in the inevitable gloom waiting to see the Roses game and this slender youth walked by carrying a cricket bag.

"Who's yon?" said the old man.

"Our new fast bowler," said the Lancashire supporter standing in front of us.

"Fast bowler," exclaimed the old man. "He's not big enough. He'll fall down before he reaches t'wicket."

The Lancashire supporter looked sheepish and stared hard at the locked gates. There was nothing he could say because the youth who passed us by was certainly the unlikeliest looking fast bowler imaginable.

The old man wasn't letting it drop there. He senses an opportunity to put the old enemy to shame.

"What's his name then?" he asked.

"Statham," said the Lancashire supporter.

"He'll get some stick today," said the man.

Two hours later we were sitting behind the bowler's arm as the new boy, spindly and pale, prepared to bowl against the might of Yorkshire. As he measured out his run the old man said, "He's not strong enough to run that far. Somebody ought to tell him."

An hour later and we were a couple of very depressed Yorkshiremen. Statham had taken the first three wickets for next to nothing, and we knew in our sinking hearts we had seen a great fast bowler in action.

Going back to Yorkshire the old man said, "Th' knows he's going to bother us that Statham."

That was seventeen years ago and in that time John Brian Statham has done everything to prove the old man right. I have never forgotten my first sight of him all those years ago and have never forgone the chance to see him in action since. Watching him through the years has been a constant pleasure. In a changing world he has remained aloof from fashion's whims, unscathed by the advance of time. Even now, at the age of thirty-seven, the figure is as lean and as pliable as in his sapling years There's the odd fleck of grey in the hair but the eyes are bright and youthful. I sought him out at Old Trafford to discover how many more seasons I might have the pleasure of watching him.

"About three more I reckon. I'd like to complete twenty years with Lancashire," he said.

What then? "Probably league cricket. Back to where I started," he said with a smile.

In the seventeen years since he left the leagues to play for Lancashire, Brian Statham has established himself as one of the truly great fast bowlers. He hasn't got the subtlety of a Lindwall, the flair of Trueman or the blasting speed of Hall. His success is based on the two classic precepts of the bowler's art: length and direction. He is the most honest of bowlers. His avowed intention is to knock all three stumps down and he never disguises the fact. In a game slowly being strangled to death by the niggardly defensive tactics of a legion of second-class seam bowlers he stands out like a bold knight at the head of a peasant army.

The nearest this gentle cautious man gets to anger is when he talks about the modern-day seam bowler, "Little phantoms" he calls them.

"They come on to bowl and they've no intention of getting a wicket. They just plop away all day, preventing the batsman from scoring, boring the crowd to death. It's wrong, terribly wrong," he said.

He shakes his head and looks out of the dressing-room window across the sunlit green of Old Trafford. The years rest lightly on him and yet one feels that perhaps Brian Statham has not reaped their full harvest. The comparison with the fortunes of Fred Trueman is inevitable if only because of their great partnership. Trueman the businessman, Trueman the journalist, Trueman the gossip columns, on the telly, Trueman in the gravy.

Brian Statham says: "I'm happy. It's a question of what you want really. Fred's different to me. He likes the limelight. I think people should be what they are. I wouldn't go on television and talk about things I knew nothing about because that's not my job. Similarly you wouldn't ask Eammon Andrews to captain Lancashire would you?"

Statham is content to remain just a very good cricketer taking only what the game offers him and not expecting more. This and his exemplary conduct on the field and off made him the ideal man to rebuild the pride and faith in Lancashire cricket. It is a daunting task. The club has bled internally in the past from dissent among the players and the committee. It has been snubbed by the cricket lovers who see no reason to accept second best after many seasons of a rich and splendid diet. At any age when, if there were any justice, he ought to be grazing in the outfield, Brian Statham is required to accomplish the most important task ever given to a Lancashire cricketer. He doesn't make any predictions. He simply says: "We'll be all right. Just wait and see."

In the three years we have left to us we ought to savour Brian Statham. The present legion of "little phantoms" who are boring us all to death should be made to watch him for a full season and then given the choice of either emulating him or retiring. Those who mourn McDonald and the Ancients should seek solace in the sight of one of the few English cricketers still playing who can stand any comparison, and those of us who write about the game should always use him as the yardstick of our judgements. In any period of the game, no matter how enriched, Statham would be a treasure. Today, even in his twilight, he is simply priceless.

Re-printed by kind permission of the Sunday Times

If They Missed, He Hit

Frank Keating remembers the greatest straight man of them all - Brian Statham of Lancashire and England in an article written for Wisden Cricket Monthly.

Only in his going did the lean, spare fellow who answered to "George" receive the approbation he had so sheepishly ducked throughout his life and his cricket. In his pomp, up the hill and into the wind, Brian Statham had lightly worn his world-wide fame; in his death, even he could not escape the universal chorus of admiration and affection.

The hymns were much warmer and more familiar in flavour than the upright and austere valedictions a twelve month before for Statham's erstwhile county captain Cyril Washbrook, the imperious opening batsman with the defiant mien. Perhaps that's because the two Lancashire legends - who probably stand highest together on the top-most plinth in the county's all -time pantheon - were definitely not two peas from the same pod. To the end Washbrook was gruffly caustic, even haughty. There was much of the Victorian mill-owner about him, whereas Statham - whose death on June 11th came just six days before his 70th birthday - never lost his confraternal and cloth-capped working man's complaisance. You could hum softly to yourself one of those corny sepia Hovis-ad brass-band melodies over a conversation with Brian.

I remember telephoning Washbrook on his 80th birthday in 1994, offering greetings on behalf of The Guardian in the hope of scrounging a few paragraphs on the state of modern cricket. I addressed him as "Sir", but was at once put in my place. "What gives your newspaper the right to telephone a complete stranger out of the blue and wish them Happy Birthday?...and good day to you, Sir!"

In contrast, telephone Brian Statham at his modest Heaton Chapel home and he was always happy for a chat on this and that and his beguiling old times. "Audrey says a natter is as good as a cure," he'd say, referring to his wife who nursed him through the stoically borne ill-health of his final years.

Statham took 252 Test wickets (briefly wrestling the all-time world record from Alec Bedser before handing it on to Fred Trueman) at 24.84 - 102 of them bowled, as testimony to the sole published maxim he uttered to his craft, "They miss, I hit." Of the wood-hitting greats only Ray Lindwall, with 42.98% of victims bowled (98 out of 228), heads Statham's 40.48%. In all, Statham took 2260 wickets at only 16.37 apiece. "And each one of those 2260 was glad to call him a friend," observed Neville Cardus. No man in history has taken more so cheaply. A quarter of Statham's nigh-on 17,000 overs were maidens; he gave away barely more than two runs an over. For Lancashire alone, he took 1816 wickets at the scarcely credible average of 15.12.

On leaving cricket, Statham at first enjoyed a rewarding and successful career with the Guinness brewing company. "For years it was the perfect job for a bloke who preferred lager," he would joke. But business is business. Guinness had to change their time-worn selling structures and affable old-time trading habits to compete with thrusting hi-tech rivals and monthly productivity printouts. Brian lost his confidence and, traumatically, found himself unable to cope. He had to take early retirement, which botched all his pension plans.

Fred Trueman, a firm and generous friend to the end, and confrère in immortal harness, once seethingly told me he reckoned he could date the overbowling of Brian to as early as 1955, only five years after his first county appearance: "Because he was that priceless commodity - the fellow who could keep an end bottled up as well as take wickets."

It was the summer after Statham's grandest tour of Australia. In the Lord's Test that year, after his new captain Peter May had asked him for 27 overs in South Africa's first innings (2 for 49), in the second he bowled 29 consecutive overs to take 7 for 39 and secure victory. In his previous match for Lancashire he had bowled 52 overs. "Then, pretty shattered by now, he had gone to Headingley and reeled off an incredible 60 overs for Peter and the team," remembered Fred. "I reckon it took him a year to recover from that passage - certainly for those poor old feet of his."

A TRIBUTE TO BRIAN STATHAM

We were boys then - and they were men. What giants they were, what craft-versed, overachieving, sun-browned heroes. We queued for their autographs and tried to copy their actions. Trueman's, of course, was the classic. There is a surviving newsreel clip of Fred's gathering, full-throttle run-up from pavilion-end mark to the crease at The Oval's fabled Test in 1953 which still takes the breath away for both hostility and aesthetics.

My first beau ideal in this regard was Gloucester's George Lambert; after the first Test I saw in 1949 Trevor Bailey - crease-jumping bob and kicked-out left leg - was the action to mime; then Fred's pluperfect glory was the one. None of us could remotely do "the Statham", which we were now seeing on fuzzy black-and-white TV. We tried, but Statham was a one-off. You had to be double-jointed to start with. There was a bounce about it, but a metronomic longish-legged lolloping bounce; 16 almost lazy strides of gathering, soft-shoed intent and, at the high point of delivery, almost a Spanish dancer's heel-click jump.

Cardus says a lot of it. "The truth about Statham's action is that it was so elastic and balanced (and double-jointed) that there was no forward shoulder-rigidity possible; his movement, from the beginning of his run to delivery, to the final accumulated propulsion, had not an awkward angle in it at all. The whole man of him was the effortless and natural dynamo and life-force of his attack."

The delivery's snaking exactness, its bullseye accuracy, was another matter. As was the uncomplaining devotion to the cause. "Oh sure," said Brian, matter-of-factly, "I'd often come off with my socks sodden with blood. Way back, Adelaide '55 I think (41 overs, 3 for 108), was the first time I had to cut out the toe of my boot. That trip my big toenail came right off. And a time or two since. Often my toes just went all black." The tale simply told; amiable, philosophic, ungrumbling.

Those could be the three watchwords for the life of the boy from Gorton who never bothered with cricket as a lad, but posted to the Midlands for National Service in the RAF, found the game excused him menial duties. However, totally uncoached, he bowled to such effect that his corporal, a Middlesex supporter, called Larry Lazarus, excitedly sent Brian's details to Lord's, who forwarded the letter to Old Trafford - where old Harry Makepeace was coach and, apparently, needed just one look.

Within three months of his demob, on his 20th birthday in 1950, Statham was opening the bowling for Lancashire against Kent. As he trod that green, green Manchester grass for the first business time that morning, Washbrook had one severe warning: "Don't bowl anything short to Arthur (Fagg), lad, 'cos he'll flog you out of sight." Now young Brian didn't know what an outswinger was, let alone a yorker, so how was he meant to know which of the Kent openers was Arthur Fagg? So he reasoned that if he dropped one short - just one - he would soon find out and take it from there. So he did, only a fraction short but a climber all right, Arthur (for it was he) went for the hook but it hurried on him...Fagg c Wharton (forward short leg) b Statham 4. He finished with 5-1-13-1, Lancashire won by an innings in two days - and in no time it was Old Trafford's rather packed Bank Holiday Roses match.

In his first over, the unheard-of stringbean hurried Hutton. Len then looked on from the bowler's end as Lowson and Lester were comprehensively bowled for ducks and Watson was snaffled by Edrich in the slips, also for 0. The colt finished with 5 for 52 and the performance lodged itself in Hutton's mind that the following winter he and Washbrook insisted that Freddie Brown send for Statham when MCC's Australian touring team needed a fast-bowling boost. Seven months after taking Fagg's wicket, he was playing his first Test at Christchurch.

By the next tour of Australia, four years later, Statham was to play a riveting part in retaining the Ashes. His captain Hutton summed up: "He was the most accurate fast bowler I ever saw. No bowler shaved the stumps more often. But never a moan or a harsh word not a black look at the umpire or captain could be associated with Brian." Never once was Statham common or mean. Never once did he bounce a tailender. "How they can stoop to such a thing these days, it defeats me? A non-bat is going to get killed soon." Once, on Hutton's tour of West Indies in 1953-54, fast bowler Frank King gashed Jim Laker's temple with a pearler. When King, a rabbit, came in to bat later, Trueman from mid-off insisted Statham answer the cruelty and let King have "one between the eyes." Brian looked across at this friend: "No, lad, the best way to hurt him is simply to clean-bowl him."

Statham and Trueman, a red rose and white, made up one of fast-bowling's grandest duos of opposite, one of the most enduring for all history. Imperturbable Brian's almost mystical control, seaming either way, with such indefatigable consistency that, on soft turf, the marks where the ball had pitched were closely grouped like a swarm of bullet-holes round the bullseye at Bisley....in glorious contrast to Fred's bullish aggro and hearty self-belief, his swing either way and his violent, volatile resource.

Oddly, for such a perfect partnership for posterity, in only half of Brian's 70 Tests was he harnessed with Fred. Statham's other grand liaison for the fabled legend, that with Frank Tyson, was only a 12-match affair - but enough to lay waste to Australia in 1954-55. (The three of them only once bowled together in a Test innings, at Adelaide in 1958-59 when Australia made 476: Statham 3 for 83, Trueman 4 for 90 and

Tyson, past his blazing peak, 1 for 100.)

Both Trueman and Tyson rush to acknowledge their partnerships' dependency on Statham. "In 15 years at the other end his accuracy ensured countless wickets for me," said Fred, "and in 50 years as true friends we never had a wrong word." said Tyson of their raging tour of Australia: "The glamour of success was mine when I captured 6 for 85 in the Sydney Test, but few spared a thought for Brian that day who bowled unremittingly for two hours into a stiff breeze and took 3 for 45. Throughout the tour I owed much to desperation injected into the batsmen's methods by Statham's relentless pursuit. To me, it felt like having Menuhin playing second fiddle to my lead."

Was it always into the wind and up the hill? I once asked. Statham smiled. "No, not always. Towards the end it was, 1962, Pakistan at Leeds. We made 500, heck of a flat pitch. Fred and I have supper on the Friday night, not relishing next day, thinking that Hanif and his brothers could bat the match out from there. Next morning, Fred comes downhill and I'm staggering up from the football-stand end into a really stiff gale. Terrible stuff. But Fred couldn't get his strides right, so he comes up to me and says, "Tell skipper we'll swap ends." And I say, "What, me have the wind and the slope, this is a first for all time, Fred." Anyway, Colin (Cowdrey) agreed, we changed ends and bowled them out twice in the day!"

In fact, Brian took 6 for 90 that day - but on the whole, like the handful of sport's most chivalrous knights, into his pained and sick old age, he preferred to talk of the deeds and nobility of the foe rather than his own. What about the 7 for 39 at Lord's (1955), you'd say, or 7 for 57 at Melbourne (1958-59), and he'd shrug: "Can't remember much about that, why not look it up in the book?" Then the eyes would glint with warm recall: "Tell you what, though, the best innings I ever saw at Lord's was 1957, Everton Weekes, absolutely brilliant, top drawer, the ridge playing up something terrible, good-length balls just taking off; he got 90 and it was utterly superb to be there watching it."

But of all he bowled to, the best was Denis Compton. "It was nothing less than genius with DCS. If it was his day you didn't stand a chance. He could play the same shot to the same delivery - and the ball could disappear into three different parts of the faraway field, simply by minutely opening or closing the angle and face of his bat."

The best ball he ever bowled? You have to drag it out of him. "Okay, Jeff Stollmeyer, good bat, Guyana Test one time (1953-54). Flat track. Pitched fractionally outside leg stump. He went to glance - and it just popped off the top of the bail. Beautiful, eh?" That was in an opening burst in which, as well as Stollmeyer for 2, he had Worrell for

0 and Walcott for 4; so at 15 for 3 in reply to England's 435, West Indies were at once heading for an innings defeat.

Both wicketkeeper Evans and Hutton, who was at slip, said that Stollmeyer's ball was the equal of Alec Bedser's peach which had dismissed Bradman at Adelaide in 1946-47, hitherto the best they'd ever seen in close-up - "though Brian's was about five times as fast," said Evans.

"George" Statham. True and utter great. The familial name among all cricket's freemasonry - and only a member could address him thus - derived from a Lancashire dressing-room habit of always having a staunch "King George". When stalwart Winston Place abdicated the name, John Brian Statham proudly assumed it. His last wicket was in the Old Trafford Roses match (Sharpe lbw b Statham 20) of August 1968 - his last over, a maiden of course, to Brian Close - and the Wisden Alamanck reported, "On each and every one of the three days the big crowds gave him standing ovations as he entered and left the field." And in his own rich thanksgiving piece, Cardus enquired: "Did Statham ever send down a wide?"

Colin Evans
Cricket correspondent of the Manchester Evening News

Brian Statham was a straightforward bloke, a quiet family man who enjoyed a pint and a fag. He also happened to be one of the world's greatest fast bowlers, but he never let that bother him too much.

Statham never boasted - his wife Audrey told me. "The nearest he got to it was after he put up some fitted wardrobes. He would lie in bed looking at them and saying 'I did a good job there' That was the only achievement I can remember him mentioning."

But he didn't have any false modesty either. His attitude was simply "I was a good bowler and I worked hard so I wasn't surprised I took so many wickets."

I once spent a Saturday morning at his Heaton Chapel home, chatting about the old days. He pulled out an old album with some rather dog-eared photos of his career, but appeared to take more pleasure in showing me the pictures of his grandchildren. It was a pleasurable three hours.

As Lancashire's president in 1997 he led a Red Rose squad to India for a one-day charity game at Eden Gardens. The heat, crowds and food of Calcutta weren't exactly to his liking, but he proved a magnificent ambassador for the club. I bumped into him one morning on a chaotic, noisy street near the party's salubrious hotel.

I was feeling sorry for myself. British Airways had lost my bags and my hastily bought, ill-fitting gear was covered in dust from the mile and a half walk from my scruffy digs on the other side of town. He put his arm around my shoulder and said. "Come and have dinner with us tonight - you can get a fairly decent pint at the Oberoi."

So I did. We had a couple of pints for the price of one in Happy Hour and it felt good to be in the company of Brian Statham.

"The Greatest of my Time"
by Trevor Bailey

Brian Statham The Greyhound

I first met Brian Statham in Sydney in 1951, when he and Roy Tattersall were flown out as replacements for Doug Wright and myself who were both on the injured list. Because of my broken thumb I was the only member of the MCC party who was in Sydney when their plane arrived, so it fell to me to look after them before they flew on to join the main group. Both were understandably pale, nervous and excited while Brian seemed very shy. That night we had our first drink together. Since then I have supped ale with him in various parts of the world and there are few better companions, cheerful, thirsty and never dull.

Statham's belated selection was very largely due to a glowing report by Len Hutton on how well he had bowled in the Roses match of the previous summer. Incidentally, this showed excellent judgement on Hutton's part,. At the time I was sceptical about sending out a young "Quickie" whose first-class experience was limited to a handful of county games. Brian was not then a truly fast bowler, being closer to fast-medium. In Australia he did not meet with a great deal of success but he was certainly not a failure while his accuracy, which was to be such a feature of his bowling, was already apparent.

Brian Statham is easy-going and rather lazy by nature, two characteristics unusual in a fast bowler. Most pacemen possess an inborn aggressiveness which helps to supply them 'bite'. Some carry their dislike for opposing batsmen to the extent of literally hating them. When a batsman has the temerity to hit them to the boundary, they think how delightful it would be if they could fell him with a bouncer. It is an understandable outlook and colleagues often deliberately try to stir up this hate relationship, but it never worked with Brian. He liked people, even opposing batsmen.

133

It is extremely irritating for a quick bowler to see a chance go down, especially if he has been pounding away for an hour or so in the heat without reward. In these circumstances some bowlers give vent to their feelings, while others simply wilt, but Brian would merely shrug his shoulders and continue with the job in hand. Of all the fast bowlers I have played with and against he remained the most imperturbable. Even when he had beaten, but not dismissed, a batsman four times in one over, as happened on one occasion on a batting paradise in the West Indies, he just gave a somewhat rueful chuckle and carried on. Not for him the extravagant gestures, the flow of colourful language and the cries to heaven for justice.

I have only seen Brian ruffled on very rare occasions. Once was at Melbourne when he had brilliantly bowled England back into the game, taking 7 for 57 in twenty-eight eight-ball overs. Justifiably, he felt he had done enough to take off his cricket boots, put on his slippers and relax with a cigarette and a glass of beer. But, alas, England batted in such a depressingly spineless fashion that we were shot out for only 87. Brian had to bat and bowl again the same day. He was not amused.

Brian Statham is often compared with his great international partner, Freddie Trueman, and inevitably there is considerable difference of opinion as to who was the finer - which does not depend upon whether you support the White or Red Rose. Tom Graveney said he preferred to bat against Brian rather than Fred. His reason was that Fred was more unpredictable. You knew, when facing Brian, exactly what to expect. In other words, Brian was a shade more accurate, but Fred more liable to produce the unplayable delivery. As far as I am concerned I do not relish facing either, but I would sooner bat against Freddie because his percentage of deliveries which I had a chance of scoring from was fractionally higher. When I was facing Brian I could never see where or how I was going to make a run. Ball after ball would pitch just short of a length on, or a fraction outside the off stump. Occasionally a delivery would appear over pitched, but it was always a designed Yorker and not the wanted half-volley.

Colin Cowdrey's reactions are identical to Graveney's and opinion among the Essex players split down the middle. Everyone prefers to have both these bowlers on their side!

Pacemen are always more formidable when they can operate in pairs. Because of his phlegmatic and unselfish approach Brian made an ideal partner. At international level he has shared the new ball with both Trueman and Tyson and both these couplings proved highly successful. Brian did not worry if he had to operate up the hill and into the wind, he simply kept on bowling fast and straight. His exceptional accuracy ensured that runs were always at a premium and was one of the main reasons why he was such a great help to his partner. The maxim of his attack has always been: if they miss I hit. Certainly over the years Brian has been indirectly responsible for a large number of wickets at the other end. On more than one occasion I have dismissed a batsman who was so delighted to have escaped temporarily from Brian that he took an unnecessary risk.

Statham has always been more of a seamer than a swing bowler, indeed even with the new ball he seldom moved it appreciably in the air. This was largely due to his body action which was, perhaps, a shade too open for the purist, but his high right arm and the way it chased his left arm across his body until checked by his left hip were copy-book. Besides being double-jointed, Brian was unusually supple, and this has helped to give him the whippy delivery which comes off the pitch a shade faster than the batsman expects. Because of his basic action, most of his deliveries tended to move into the right-handed batsman, but occasionally he made one leave off the seam. He bowled an utterly bemused Jeff Stollmeyer with just such a ball on a perfect pitch in a Caribbean Test. It pitched around middle and leg and clipped the top of the off. It would have bowled anyone in the world; a broth of a ball.

Unlike many fast bowlers, Statham has never been "bouncer happy." He used the bumper as a very occasional shock ball, and if I were to make a criticism I would say that it might have profited him sometimes to have tried a few more. He also did not believe in letting the "tail" have one, as he reckoned he ought to be able to bowl them without recourse to fear and violence. He was usually right, but again it might have occasionally paid to have slipped in a bouncer when they were proving unusually obdurate and holding up the proceedings.

Watching Brian stride forth to bat was always one of cricket's happier moments. On the way he would normally pause to pass a few pleasantries with the opposition, before taking a largely perfunctory guard. He would next somewhat optimistically scan the more remote areas of the ground and then was prepared to do battle. His innings might not last long, but it was usually entertaining. Brian was an unconventional left-handed bat with a good eye, who relied mainly on aggressive strokes and did not believe in getting behind the line. His defence was almost entirely limited to a somewhat diffident forward push, but his attacking shots were varied and colourful, including a delightfully rustic mow to leg, a surprisingly classical cover drive, a powerful slash, and an absolutely invaluable edge, both inside and out. On one never-to-be-forgotten occasion in the fourth Test in South Africa, Brian, in partnership with Peter Loader, gave a superb exhibition of "edge-manship" against Heine and Adcock with the new ball. For forty-eight minutes they snicked 'em here and they snicked 'em there, until I was close to tears and the opposing bowlers to apoplexy.

Brian's supple build and speed over the ground, combined with a wonderful throwing arm, made him an exceptional outfielder. In addition he had a superb pair of hands. Once the ball was in the air and he was anywhere in the vicinity the bowler could afford to relax.

Statham possessed two nicknames, "Greyhound" and "George". The former was doubtless derived from his pace over the ground, loping stride and lean appearance. In his early days he looked deceptively slight, although he always weighed considerably more than people imagined. The origin of "George" is somewhat obscure, but it suited him. "George", after all, is a friendly, homely name and Brian is essentially a friendly, homely person - indeed as far as Brian was concerned, the one serious snag about touring overseas was the long time he had to be away from his family and the home he loved.

I cannot recall anyone who did not like Statham as an individual, as well as admiring him as a bowler. This is rare in a sport which is frequently cut-throat and where somewhat malicious gossip flourishes. It followed that Brian made a wonderful tourist. He was even-tempered, enjoyed his food and his ale, threw a nifty dart, relished an informal party, especially one where he could remove his shoes, and never caused anyone any trouble. In addition he possessed a keen sense of humour and a dry wit. He had the habit of producing a succinct comment on life in general when, for example, we were just about to board a plane at some uncivilised hour in the morning. He was prepared to saunter leisurely, and not too seriously, around a golf course, though he preferred a putting green, liked a game of tennis, at which he was distinctly useful, and appreciated a day at the races whether he won or lost. Perhaps he was a shade lacking in ambition, but he possessed that priceless virtue, charity.

He was never by nature, or inclination, an enthusiastic trainer. Neither Brian nor I was ever able to raise much enthusiasm for P.T. on board ship and we both found deck quoits infinitely more satisfactory than the energetic deck tennis.

I have always enjoyed nets, at least when they are well organised and without doubt Brian was my favourite net bowler. I have always taken strong exception to being hit while practising and therefore will not face anyone likely to do this. On the Len Hutton tour I refused to have Frank Tyson in my net, because his length was not altogether trustworthy, but Brian Statham of course was accuracy personified. He was prepared to send down any type of ball the batsman required and helped me enormously. He himself seldom bothered about batting in the nets unless specially commanded.

Brian was endowed with a wiry toughness and a stamina which enabled him to bowl long spells without too much strain. He kept fit by bowling, rather than by training in order to be fit to bowl. Because he could keep going for over after over without losing much of either his pace or his accuracy and because he never moaned, there was an understandable tendency to bowl him too much. Fortunately his vitality allowed him to recover remarkably quickly from this mistreatment. However, on one occasion it did leave its mark. This was at Lord's in 1955. As usual he had already sent down a goodly quantity of overs for Lancashire and England that season, when he was called upon to bowl unchanged throughout the whole of the South African second innings. He finished with 7 wickets for 39 overs. I doubt whether he has ever bowled better and it rates as one of the great sustained fast bowling feats. It won us the match, but it was a year before Brian was quite himself again.

It is always an asset if a member of a touring party has a party piece which he can trot out on the appropriate occasion. Brian Statham's particular accomplishment was decidedly unusual and considerably more wholesome than most! He had the ability, at any hour of the night, to make the most delicious pancakes. He tossed these with the nonchalance of a super-chef and his drops were even fewer than on the cricket field. I have sampled his pancakes in all parts of the world and at the oddest times, but for the moment suprême I would choose an evening in Australia when he was given the freedom of any army kitchen with scores of eggs and gallons of milk at his disposal. He went on for over after over and must have produced enough to satisfy a battalion. I have never eaten quite so many pancakes at one sitting!

From Playfair Cricket Monthly, May 1966

Statham of Lancashire
by Brian Bearshaw

Statham made his debut for Lancashire in 1950. He was the fast bowler Lancashire had been waiting for since Ted McDonald had retired nearly 20 years earlier and he was to provide the spearhead of the county attack for 19 summers.

His Test career was launched only months after first playing for Lancashire when he was flown out to Australia and New Zealand to join the MCC party. He played in 70 Tests and took 252 wickets, which was a record at the time; he played 430 times for Lancashire and his 1,816 wickets is a record for the county.

Statham was a down-to-earth solid Northerner, beautifully typified by a story told by former England and Middlesex off-spinner Fred Titmus, who was with Statham on the 1962-3 tour of Australia.

"We went by boat and Ted Dexter, who was captain, said to us: "I don't care what you do, lads, but one meal we are going to have is breakfast. It's the most important meal of the day." So everybody had breakfast for 10 days.

Brian had not been able to leave with us and travelled by air to Perth where we all joined up. Things were explained to him, including the rule...everybody has breakfast. Brian said "What! I've never had breakfast in my life and I don't intend starting now. A cigarette and a coffee, that's my breakfast." And that was the end of breakfast for everybody on the tour."

The most memorable of the Old Trafford Tests in which Statham played was that of 1956 when off-spinner Jim Laker took 19 Australian wickets.

"My only contribution was to catch Richie Benaud on the edge," he smiled. "There wasn't much grass on the wicket but I never saw it as a vicious turner. It wasn't a really naughty wicket - they just didn't bat too well." He recalled the 1961 Test against Australia when Richie Benaud bowled England to defeat. "Ted Dexter had batted well and virtually won the game on his own. But Richie bowled beautifully and I remember Brian Close came in for some criticism when he was caught sweeping.

"I don't think Closey had taken enough care. He had just hit a four and Norman O'Neill, who had gone for the ball, had not got back to his position.

"Close swept and was caught and perhaps he was not as vigilant as he should have been as to where the fielders were positioned. It's the sort of shot that's a good one if it goes for four, a bad one if you get out."

One day in 1972 I took some wickets - well, 6-24, as if I'd forgotten! - in a colts match. At the tea interval I was told to go out and bowl in the 1st XI trial straight afterwards. I duly did so, took off my sweater and handed it to the umpire, Brian Statham. I felt like an interior decorator giving his brush for Picasso to hold.

Scyld Berry
Sunday Telegraph

Tributes from the Internet

I first saw Brian bowl when my dad took me to Old Trafford in about 1959. I was 10 years old, that day made a massive impression on my life. Brian became and still is my sporting hero. Today's county players are pretenders by comparison. **David Fare**

I watched him from beyond the boundary but even from safe haven I was aware that he was ferocious in bowling but friendly in manner. The game, battered and bruised by contemporary corruption has lost a pillar of poise, principle and panache. **Laurie Foster**

I can well remember watching him when I was a young man and being impressed with both his skill a a bowler and his demeanour on the field - quiet and undemonstrative. For those of us who recall those days of old when the great game was unsullied by rampant commercialism and venal players, memories of the likes of Statham offer in these 'troubles' much to look back with gratitude. **Osmund Perera**

I have great memories of Brian Statham - at primary school my best friend was his nephew and we used to go to Old Trafford to watch Lancashire. Brian Statham was the most consistent bowler I have seen. **David Lewis**

I first saw Brian Statham on TV during the 1957 West Indies tour of England. The next year my father took me to Lord's to see my first Test match with England playing India. I was treated to the greatest sight imaginable which left a lasting impression on me, Freddie Trueman was bowling at one end and Brian at the other. Statham had the most magnificent flowing run up and rhythmical action I have ever seen. He was probably the most accurate bowler of his type ever to play the game. The story is told that whilst undergoing a fitness test whilst on tour in Australia he hit a single stump nineteen times out of twenty four balls bowled. For me Brian was the greatest, someone to try and copy, a real hero. I have not seen his like since and I probably never will. **Julian Denny**

Accuracy = Brian Statham **Ashwin Singh**

As a Yorkshireman of 51, I spent my youth in the great Statham/Trueman days but unlike my friends I favoured Brian and he became my hero. His run to the wicket and his accuracy and no fuss approach will always be remembered. He often seemed unlucky-balls missing the stumps etc. but he never complained. A true hero. **Steve Marsh**

In my opinion, he was the best fast bowler I have ever seen. The fluidity of his delivery. I journeyed from the USA specifically to attend an occasion for him at the Grosvenor House in London organised mostly by another great bowler Trueman. **James Babb**

Brian Statham was one of the best medium-fast bowlers of the fifties and early sixties. Together with Fred Trueman they were a formidable team indeed. We will always cherish the wonderful memories, especially in the West Indies. **Sat and Tull Ramlakhan**

I remember watching Brian Statham bowling for England in tandem with Freddie Trueman, Brian had a wonderful rhythm and accuracy. I had the pleasure of seeing him in the flesh just once playing for Lancs at Liverpool when he was bowled first ball, the day after he had been dropped by England! A great player and gentleman. **Tony Heron**

As a young man growing up in the West Indies, Grenada, I followed his career with great interest. The game has lost one of its greatest. **David Paul**

I grew up on a diet of radio cricket description in rural Australia at a time when Brian Statham and Fred Trueman formed the most effective opening combination in world cricket. Brian Statham will be remembered for his sportsmanship and unselfish contribution to our great game. **Bill Yates**

Brian was a gentleman to the core. Cricket today need men of his calibre. **Omkar Persaud**

Having grown up in Stockport in the 1950s Brian Statham was the bowler we all wanted to emulate. I have never heard anyone with a bad word to say about "George," cricket has lost a great ambassador. **Eric Alcock**

I had the privilege of working with the late Jackie McGlew who stated categorically that in his opinion "George" was the finest fast bowler he had ever seen. **Roy Webster**

A truly resilient and great fast bowler of his time who provided invaluable support to

A TRIBUTE TO BRIAN STATHAM

Fred Trueman. I remember the late John Arlott describing Brian Statham in all his glory as he battled Richie Benaud's Aussies in the early 60s - bowling to Neil Harvey and bowling him out at Lord's during a Test Match - a truly remarkable BBC moment in all its glory! A true gentleman, Brian Statham. **Pingle Reddy**

My all time favourite sportsman and cricketer. The most unassuming person you could meet, but the most reliable and successful bowler, who always got his "Bucket" hands to those swirling catches. **Tim Clarkson**

The cricketing world has lost one of the finest bowlers. It is hard to forget his final stride of little hop, jump and delivery. Of all batsmen the English have sent on tour to India, Statham as a bowler stood in my memory. As a young lad I saw Brian coming to the pavilion at Chepauk with face so red from the humid Madras heat. These memories still are alive. **B Vittaldas Baliga**

As a young Yorkshire cricket-mad boy I used to go to the Test matches at Headingley with my father. I hoped that England would lose the toss on the first morning so I could watch Statham and Trueman bowl. Even as a Yorkshireman I have always admired Mr Statham as one of the greatest opening bowlers I have ever seen. **Brian Wells**

As a boy and even now, I've always held him in the highest of esteem. I shall miss him. I used to follow the commentary with so much of delight and that tremendous accuracy with which he used to deliver the ball. **Ali Khan**

Though I was only born seven years after Brian Statham stopped playing, there was no cricketer I had greater respect for. He epitomised all that cricket should be about, and in doing so highlighted all that is wrong with player's attitudes today. His record speaks for itself. **Andrew Sheldon**

One of my childhood heroes who did so much to give me a love of cricket. The style, the accuracy, but above all the sportsmanship and basic decency should be the legacy that so many should strive to emulate. **John Grant**

I have so many fond memories of Brian, who epitomised all that was good about Lancashire and England cricket. Many times I 'wagged' school to wander over to Old Trafford to watch my idol in action. I always had a great thrill when he took a wicket and I watched all his Tests at his home ground. Since emigrating to NZ in 1974, I have kept in touch with my beloved county and followed Brian's involvement in the club since his retirement. Brian was regularly compared with two other greats down here, namely Ray Lindwall and Richard Hadlee, which is praise indeed. **Pat Bindon**

A true gentleman of the game - and one hell of a player. It's an overused phrase, but we really won't see the likes of him again. **Ian Travis**

I had the pleasure of watching him bowl in Jamaica where I am from, also in England where I resided for 11 years. As a club cricketer and fellow fast bowler I learned a lot just watching him. **Cyril Logan**

When I was in Uganda I used to skip school so I could listen to commentaries when Brian the gentleman George was bowling for England. I have fond and happy memories and will treasure them as long as I live. **Shiraz Ialani**

Freddie Trueman was absolutely right. Brian Statham was a fine cricketer, a very good team player and a gentleman. **Derek de Sa**

Reproduced by kind permission of CricInfo

Bibliography

Brian Statham by Geoff Wilde.
Association of Cricket Statisticians & Historians 1993.
Brian Statham's Benefit Brochure, edited by John Kay. 1961.
From The Stretford End, by Brian Bearshaw. Partridge Press 1990.
Wisden Cricket Monthy. The Cricketer. Playfair Cricket Monthly.
Lancashire CCC Yearbook 1950-2001.
England Test Cricketers, by Bill Frindall. Willow Books 1989.
Brian Statham, by Tony Derlien Breeden Books 1990.
Cricket Merry-Go-Round, by Brian Statham. Stanley Paul. 1956.
Flying Bails, by Brian Statham. Stanley Paul 1961.
A Spell at the Top, by Brian Statham. Souvenir Press. 1969.
The Book of Cricket Lists, Edited by Norman Giller. Future 1984.
100 Yorkshire Greats by Mick Pope & Paul Dyson.Tempus. 2001.
100 Warwickshire Greats, by Robert Brooke. Tempus. 2001.
100 Glamorgan Greats, by Andrew Hignell. Tempus. 2000.
County print cards, Text by William Powell.
The Greatest of my Time, by Trevor Bailey Eyre & Spottiswoode 1968.

His ability to toss the World's best pancakes at any hour of the night was somewhat overshadowed by his International reputation as the most accurate of fast bowlers.

Roy ULLYETT.